Global 2000: Canada

Global 2000: Canada

A View of Canadian Economic Development Prospects, Resources and the Environment

By

Roger D. Voyer
Nordicity Group Ltd.
&
Mark G. Murphy
MGM Research Associates

This study was commissioned at the initiative of Environment Canada and its publication sponsored by the Canadian Association for the Club of Rome.

Pergamon Press
Toronto • Oxford • New York • Sydney • Paris • Frankfurt

Pergamon Press Offices:

Canada	Pergamon Press Canada Ltd., Suite 104, 150 Consumers Road, Willowdale, Ontario, Canada M2J 1P9
U.K.	Pergamon Press Ltd., Headington Hill Hall, Oxford, OX3 0BW, England
U.S.A.	Pergamon Press Inc., Maxwell House, Fairview Park, Elmsford, New York 10523, U.S.A.
Australia	Pergamon Press (Aust.) Pty. Ltd., P.O. Box 544, Potts Point, N.S.W. 2011, Australia
France	Pergamon Press SARL, 24 rue des Ecoles, 75240 Paris, Cedex 05, France
Federal Republic of Germany	Pergamon Press GmBh, Hammerweg 6, 6242 Kronberg-Taunus, Federal Republic of Germany

Canadian Cataloguing in Publication Data
Voyer, Roger, 1938–
    Global 2000: Canada

Includes index.
Bibliography: p.
ISBN 0-08-025418-7 (bound). — ISBN 0-08-025419-5 (pbk.)

1. Canada - Economic conditions - 1971–   *
2. Canada - Economic policy - 1971–   *   3. Economic forecasting - Canada.   4. Natural resources -
Canada.   I. Murphy, Mark G.   II. Title.

HC115.V69   1984   330.971′0646   C84-099081-2

Printed and Bound in Canada

Contents

Appendices

Preface

The *Global 2000 Report to the President* of the United States and the subsequent study *Global 2000: Implications for Canada* posed some of the critical questions facing all societies in moving toward the 21st Century. The study "Global 2000, Implications for Canada", was prepared primarily for Environment Canada and it reflects the department's active interest and involvement in a search for prosperous and sustainable development.

These earlier reports clearly revealed the complex interdependencies in our economic and social development that affect the environment and, conversely, that are affected by the environment. Sustainable development will follow from the wise and judicious deployment of environmental resources, a deployment which takes full account of the vital interactions and interdependencies between market activities and the environment.

The content and conclusions of this report are provided by the authors as contributions to the further explorations of our actions for the future. The continuing study of the issues raised, and the closer integration of our scientific and environmental knowledge with economic decisions is strongly encouraged. The practical policy decisions we face each day demand a far wider extension of both national and international dialogues and activities, if we are to ensure that our future combines prosperous economic and social progress with a healthy environment.

Executive Summary

This study looks at Canada from an internal perspective. In this way it complements an earlier study, *Global 2000: Implications for Canada*, which provided a "view from the outside" on Canada by the authors of the Global 2000 Report to the President of the United States. The study takes a structural, or long term, perspective on issues facing Canada; a perspective which is gaining acceptance in economic and decision-making circles.

Firstly, when situating Canada within the international economy (Chapters 3 and 4) one sees a small open economy having grown increasingly dependent on the US economy in the post-war period, even in more recent years when the US experienced a relative decline vis-à-vis other countries. Moreover, Canada has continued to depend on resource exports for economic health and has not evolved with other industrial countries towards higher value-added industries. This phenomenon, combined with unique levels of foreign-ownership in our resource and manufacturing industries, has resulted in a serious balance of international payments situation, where resource exports are increasingly needed to offset a rapidly increasing service account deficit.

In analyzing the Canadian economy sectorally (Chapter 5), there are bright spots such as the service sector and within that sector, tourism. However, resources remain a cornerstone of the economy. The resource sector faces deep structural problems, however, be they related to the limits of the resource base as in agriculture, the environment, such as the acid rain question related to resource processing or to social issues such as in the Atlantic fishery, problems which can only be corrected over the longer term, if Canada's resources are to serve us in the future as they have in the past.

Moreover, the Canadian economy has increasingly become more fragmented as provinces undertook an active role in economic and industrial development within their boundaries to create employment opportunities for their constituents (Chapter 6). Increasing provincial involvement in the economy is in part the result of the perceived limitations of the federal government to effect changes that are in keeping with provincial needs. These needs range from creation of employment for a growing labour force to the social requirements of an aging society in a growing urban environment (Chapter 7).

Economic decision-making in Canada is highly politicized because of the size and power of the three major actors involved in the decision-making process: government (two levels), business and labour, which in Canada form an uneasy alliance at best (Chapter 8). Because of the lack of consensus on economic directions among these actors, the onus falls on the federal government to provide leadership (Chapter 9). An essential element of this federal leadership will be the need to engage business and labour in discussions of economic directions. This will necessitate a form of "indicative planning" as the substrate on which discussions can take place if Canada is to keep pace with other industrialized countries. Out of this dialogue should come directions for economic development leading to needed structural changes. Since these structural changes can only be brought about slowly over time, an economic development strategy will have to be set in place and sustained to the year 2000 and beyond to minimize the stresses that a fundamental economic re-structuring entails.

The strategy to guide Canada to the year 2000 and beyond should include the following elements:

- continued emphasis on resource development into the medium term with an acceptance of attendant social and environmental stresses for balance of payments reasons;

- setting in place and sustaining a long-term industrial strategy based on;

    a) capturing new industrial (particularly high-technology) opportunities;

    b) import replacement; and

    c) developing goods and services related to priorities such as urbanization and an aging population. Specific areas for action should come from the indicative planning exercise referred to earlier;

- Setting in place policies to tap Canadian capital markets more effectively and to encourage the development of Canadian-owned establishments to reduce the deficit on the service account;

- developing policies that would ensure a sustainable resource base as well as support appropriate resource and industrial development and implement them as the pressure on balance of payments eases in the medium term and beyond; and,

- investigating new approaches to employment, such as a shorter work week, working from the home, work-sharing and so on, that maintain an acceptable standard of living.

Such a strategy would catalyze industrial re-structuring and minimize the stresses which are now apparent. This approach should, of course, be cast within a broader framework, which recognizes "total costing" that reveals the real costs of stresses on the resource base and the environment.

Foreword

In view of increasing concerns expressed by numerous experts through-out the world about global resource depletion, population growth and economic disparities, President Carter, in his Environmental Message to the Congress of May 23, 1977, directed the Council on Environmental Quality and the Department of State, working with other federal agencies, to study the "probable changes in the world's population, natural resources and environment to the end of the century." This endeavour was to serve as "the foundation of our longer term planning."

In response to this directive, *The Global 2000 Report to the President* was published in Washington, D.C. in mid-1980.

At the initiative of Environment Canada and with financial contributions from other Federal Government Departments and Agencies, Dr. Gerald O. Barney and Associates Inc., the same firm retained by the U.S. Government to manage and direct the preparation of their study, was commissioned to assess the *Global 2000: Implications for Canada*, in the form of "a view from the outside" and "to provide a starting point for further dialogue and action." Publication of the Report was sponsored by the Canadian Association for the Club of Rome and was financially supported by prominent Canadian business companies.

The wide ranging interest that was shown in the evolving discussions throughout Canada encouraged the Department of the Environment to solicit further contributions to the dialogue and thus the report *Global 2000: Canada; A View of Canadian Economic Development Opportunities, Resources and the Environment*, was commissioned.

This study now complements the earlier *Global 2000: Implications for Canada* by looking at Canada's future not as seen from the outside by the authors of the Report to the President of the United States, but from a Canadian focussed internal perspective.

The purpose of this report is to encourage further serious consideration of the questions raised and to facilitate the disaggregation of overall findings and contentions to the point where the issues become relevant and indeed important to regional and sectoral decision-making and policies.

The intent of this study, as with the earlier studies, is to offer some further insight and perceptions, which can focus attention upon the complexity of the issues and their strategic implications. Active participation by all concerned, both in locations across Canada and by sectoral interests, should help to promote better understanding and at least some greater mutual respect for views, where genuine conflict emerge.

The general initiative that has now been launched by Environment Canada to foster discussions and better understandings, continues to generate enouraging responses and interactions between various actors and interest groups.

The report should thus be viewed as a renewed invitation to all concerned to contribute their skills and expertise to the improvement of our knowledge base that is to help in better addressing the practical policy decision that we face and which demand a wider extension of national as well as international dialogues and efforts. We wish to thank Environment Canada for the opportunity of preparing this study. The views expressed here are ours and do not necessarily reflect those of the sponsor.

Roger Voyer
Mark Murphy

1. Background

a) The Global 2000 Report to the President of the U.S.A.

In view of increasing concerns expressed by numerous experts throughout the world about global resource depletion, population growth and economic disparities, President Carter, in his Environmental Message to the Congress of May 23, 1977, directed the Council on Environmental Quality and the Department of State, working with other federal agencies, to study the "probable changes in the world's population, natural resources and environment to the end of the century." This endeavour was to serve as "the foundation of our longer term planning."

In response to this directive, *The Global 2000 Report to the President* was published in Washington, D.C. in mid-1980. The study concluded that:

- Rapid world population growth will continue, mostly in the poorest countries. GNP per capita will remain low in most less-developed countries (LDCs) and the gap between rich and poor nations will widen.

- World food production will increase 90 percent from 1970 to 2000, but the bulk of the increase will go to countries with already high per capita food consumption. Real food prices will double.

- Arable land will increase only 4 percent by 2000, and most of the increased food output will have to be from higher yields, which will mean increasingly heavy dependence on oil.

- World oil production will reach maximum estimated capacity, even with rapidly increasing prices. Many LDCs will have difficulties meeting energy needs. Fuel-wood demands will exceed supplies by 25 percent.

- Mineral resources will meet projected demands, but production costs will increase and the 25 percent of world population in industrial countries will continue to absorb 75 percent of world mineral production.

- Regional water shortages will become more severe. Population growth alone will double water requirements in nearly half the world and deforestation in many LDCs will make water supplies increasingly erratic.

- There will be significant losses of world forests as demand for forest products increases. Growing stocks of commercial-size timber are projected to decline 50 percent per capita. By 2000, 40 percent of the remaining forest cover in LDCs will be gone.

1

- There will be serious world-wide deterioration of agricultural soils. The spread of desert-like conditions is likely to accelerate.

- Atmospheric concentrations of carbon dioxide and ozone-depleting chemicals will increase at rates that could alter the world's climate and upper atmosphere significantly by 2050. Acid rain will continue to damage lakes, soils and crops.

- Extinction of plant and animal species will increase dramatically and 20 percent of all species on earth may be irretrievably lost as their habitats vanish, especially in tropical forests.

Thus, *The Global 2000 Report* concludes that vigorous, determined, new initiatives are needed if worsening poverty and human suffering, environmental degradation and international tension and conflicts are to be prevented. There are no quick fixes. The only solutions to the problems of population, resources and environment are complex and long-term. These problems are inextricably linked to some of the most perplexing and persistent problems in the world—poverty, injustice and social conflict. An era of unprecedented co-operation and commitment is essential. The available evidence leaves no doubt that the world faces enormous, urgent and complex problems in the decades immediately ahead. Prompt and vigorous changes in public policy around the world are needed now. Long lead times are required for effective action.

b) The Canadian Future: A View from the Outside

In 1980 Environment Canada, with financial contributions from other federal departments and agencies, commissioned Dr. Gerald O. Barney and Associates Inc., the firm which directed the study for the U.S. Government, to assess the GLOBAL 2000: IMPLICATIONS FOR CANADA. That study comprised "a view from the outside" that was designed "to provide a starting point for further dialogue and action." Publication of that Report was sponsored by the Canadian Association for the Club of Rome and was financially supported by prominent Canadian companies.

The analysis of the implications for Canada of the findings in the *Global 2000 Report* suggests that in the midst of gloomy global developments, Canada can be expected to face a relatively bright future: its resources are evidently ample to meet the needs of a population even in excess of 30 million, although it is to be realized that in comparison to global demands, the supplies are totally inadequate. Nevertheless it is apparent that there will be increasing pressures upon Canada for ever greater supplies to the rest of the world of basic resources, such as food, energy, forest products, minerals, which in turn will place increasing stress upon land, air and water resources in the country. In these circumstances there is evident need for concerted attention to the wise use of resources in Canada that will ensure that the exploitation of natural wealth will be dictated by longer term national/global interests rather than short-term gains or political expedience. Such prudence in the development and supply of resources to the rest of the world will inevitably demand some very hard choices and responsible stewardship as well as the careful protection of environmental resources and of sustainable resource yields.

Specifically, the *Global 2000: Implications for Canada* study concludes that relative to many other nations, Canada faces a promising future insofar as the nation has:

- a well-educated population and is not overpopulated.

- a large (albeit not wholly domestically owned) capital base and a high income and GNP per capita.

- abundant and relatively inexpensive food supplies.

- abundant and relatively stable forests.

- abundant mineral and energy resources to meet its own needs and is thus much less dependent on foreign energy supplies than many other nations.

- relatively few environmental problems compared with many other countries, even though there are severe problems with acid rain and some potentially difficult agricultural soil and water problems.

- is unlikely to be invaded or isolated from its largest trade partner.

- can expect increasing interest in its resources.

Notwithstanding these favourable conditions, Canada does face some vulnerabilities and comparative disadvantages:

- it is largely a resource exporting economy and therefore needs trading partners as a base for a strong economy.

- immigration pressures will increase.

- it may approach the limit of its grain export potential before the end of the century.

- it remains vulnerable to climatic changes.

- it may continue to experience some internal tensions that relate to resource development policies.

The biggest threat to Canada may be the disturbance of its economy because of dislocations in the global economy. As an open, resource exporting country, Canada is vulnerable to economic dislocations in the rest of the world that are likely to occur in the years ahead, e.g., balance of payments problems, protectionism, financial and other economic calamities. Also, a cooling of the world's climate (or even a few years of adverse weather in Canada) could seriously increase Canada's vulnerability to any economic disruptions taking place in other parts of the world.

Global economic problems resulting from population growth, resource (especially oil) depletion and environmental deterioration will thus be very large indeed over the coming decades. Even with unprecedented co-operation among nations, it will be difficult for Canada to protect itself to any extent from excessive economic vulnerability while still playing a responsible role as a leading nation.

c) Economic Development Prospects, Resources and the Environment

Against the above "view from the outside," this study now examines issues from a Canadian focussed internal perspective. While the general conclusions reached essentially correspond to those identified in the earlier documents, the analysis of the overall findings are carried several steps forward. Because of the emphasis placed upon an analysis of the structure of the Canadian economy, some of the deeper and possibly even intractable problems facing Canadians may be better identified.

It is hoped that by focussing in this report on specific economic, resource and environmental stresses facing Canadian decision-makers, it will be possible to raise concrete issues and the level of public debate against the background of a systematic analytical framework, that is to guide Canadian policies and actions to the year 2000 and beyond.

2. Introduction

The 1970s caught most economic managers in the industrialized countries of the world by surprise; traditional government economic policies were found to have but limited success in dealing with unusual inflationary, monetary and unemployment conditions. The frustrations experienced have led some observers to look for new approaches to economic and social problems.

An alternative approach to economic development planning adopted a more systematic *structural* analysis of the economy. This effort focusses attention upon those aspects of the economy that change only slowly over time, such as the sectoral make-up, human skills, institutions and so on, and on the formulation of policies that would result in a more sustainable economic growth through structural adjustment to new and innovative activities. This approach is in contrast to traditional market demand oriented economics, which claims that the management of economic growth, by means of fiscal/monetary policies, will bring about such structural changes in the economy as may be required.

The confrontation between what are termed "supply-side" and "demand-side" economics respectively has generated a heated debate among economists, largely because the advocates of the former stance accept government intervention while the latter favour reliance on free-market mechanisms for economic progress. Discussions by OECD, beginning as early as the 1970s, reflected the difficulty of reconciling the two points of view as evidenced by the following statements:

> "We have emphasized in this report the long-term "structural" nature of some of those problems which today confront the OECD Member countries, and the limitations of short-term demand management strategies in tackling them."[1]

and,

> "Positive adjustment also requires coherence of macro and micro-economic policies. Non-accommodating monetary and fiscal policies are self-defeating if at the same time they allow industry, manpower and micro-economic policies to contribute to the preservation of inefficient economic structures."[2]

In its study, "INTERFUTURES" the OECD concluded that:

> "While demand management is by no means out-of-date, the various long-term economic concerns which we have been able to

5

identify . . . all point to the *growing prominence of supply considerations in the future political agendas.* More precisely, our analyses
suggest that developed economies are entering a lengthy and turbu-
lent period of adjustment to changing relative scarcities in their
factor endowment, with natural resources and capital in shorter
supply and labour more abundant."[3]

The structural approach to economic development planning has become
more widely accepted because there is a growing apprehension that short-term
palliatives cannot deal effectively with more deeply entrenched problems. For
example, the Japan Federation of Economic Organizations[4] and the Netherlands Scientific Council for Government Policy[5] have undertaken structural
analyses of their respective economies. In Canada, the debate between the
Science Council and the Economic Council in the 1970s on appropriate
industrial development policies reflected a "structuralist" versus "traditional-
ist" perspective.[6]

The Canadian Institute for Economic Policy (CIEP), set in place in 1979,
advocated an alternative "structuralist" view in the economic debate. In the
words of CIEP:

"... there is a growing movement in Canada and abroad advocating
a return to laissez-faire. The message of this conventional wisdom is
very simple. Free trade, particularly with the United States, will
solve Canada's structural difficulties. Governments should cut their
expenditures and balance their budgets. Until this objective is
achieved and inflation is curbed, the expansion of the money supply
should be restricted and high interest rates should be maintained. To
the extent that the exercise of private monopoly power leads to
rising prices, a more active competition policy should be pursued.
Free collective bargaining, as developed during the post-war period
in North America, should continue to determine wage structures
and other conditions of work. Multinational corporations should be
free to expand where and how they wish. In other words, unfettered
private enterprise and private investment should become the prime
movers of industrialized economies.

These remedies are appealing in their simplicity. But they
cannot cope with the new economic realities. Canada now faces a
period in which new technologies are displacing employment, older
technologies are reaching maturity, population growth is abating,
more women are joining the labour market, and more people wish to
buy foreign products and travel abroad. For these reasons and
others, if laissez-faire prevails, Canadians will continue to suffer
from limited private investment opportunities, slower growth, and
continued inflation.

There is accordingly an urgent need in Canada, and elsewhere, to challenge the conventional wisdom. Other views and policy prescriptions must be formulated and diffused. Canadians must have the opportunity to look at alternatives in order to make the best choices."[7]

This study focusses upon a more detailed structural analysis of the economy for the identification of issues, problems and opportunities in Canada in order to contribute to the development of a suitable background and framework for policy consideration.

References

1. OECD: *Technical Change and Economic Policy*, Paris 1980; p. 106.
2. Michalski W: Head of OECD's Planning and Evaluation Unit in an article in the *OECD Observer*, November 1982.
3. OECD: INTERFUTURES FUT(77) s.17, 1977; p.75.
4. Japan Federation of Economic Organizations; *The Japanese Economy, its Present Phase and Medium-Term Tasks*, 1979.
5. Netherlands Scientific Council for Government Policy: *Industry in the Netherlands; its Place and Future*, 1980 (English 1982).
6. see French, R.: *How Ottawa Decides*, Canadian Institute for Economic Policy, 1980.
7. Canadian Institute for Economic Policy; *Out of Joint with the Times*, 1979; p.11.

3. The New International Economic Environment

The post-war years have been a period of unparalleled economic growth. It was during this period that most of the world's industrial capacity was created and that the USA and the USSR emerged as super-powers.

The USA emerged from World War II as the undisputed economic power. The conditions for the operation of the post-war world economy were organized under international auspices dominated by the USA (e.g., World Bank, Marshall Plan). The political situation in Europe, vis-à-vis the USSR, also relied on American political as well as economic leadership.

Furthermore, the reorganization of the world economy, under American influence, affected the relationships between developed and developing countries. The less developed countries (LDCs) became progressively more intensely integrated into the general network of world markets, thus loosening the preferences, which, in the past, benefited primarily the former colonial powers.

Rapid economic development in Europe and Japan, the emergence of the Third World as an economic force and increased East-West trade are all leading to readjustments in the balance of political and economic power throughout the world. With competition now increasing, the pre-eminence of the USA is being seriously challenged. Canada, like other industrialized countries, is similarly facing a period of new uncertainties that may call for fundamentally new approaches to international relations.

a) The emergence of organized markets and trading blocs

The economic policies of most countries, during the post-war period, including Canada, were designed to stimulate rapid economic expansion. The objective was to achieve and sustain a high and stable level of employment and income. Governments began to play an increasingly significant role in economic development. They allocated resources to stimulate industrial and regional development and to cover infrastructure costs; they regulated overall economic activity by means of the then new Keynesian fiscal and monetary policies while on the social side, they increased spending on such services as public health, education and welfare. Increasingly, the modern industrial state has become characterized by more intervention and direction for both economic and social purposes.

Post-war economic expansion led to increasing interaction and trade among countries. Direct American and European (and latterly Japanese) investment in various countries has led to increasing integration of the world economy, while stimulating dependence on and trade in Western types of goods and services.

The prime agents of economic dominance, that emerged during this period, through direct foreign investment, have been the large and powerful transnational or multinational firms. These firms, because of their level of integration, are now able to influence the economic activities and policies of governments in host countries and elsewhere. Their activities are determined less and less by competition and free market forces. As a matter of fact they have frustrated the operations of the free market by virtually eliminating the price mechanism in any market through their ability to shift incomes and profits by such procedures as transfer pricing between their subsidiaries and/or cross-subsidizing activities in different industries. Many of these firms now hold substantial investments throughout the world and, given the mobility of activities to areas, where factors of production are available on favourable conditions, they can deploy their resources on a world-wide basis so as to maximize their effectiveness by seeking out those countries with the most advantageous business environment. This flexibility often tends to loosen the firm's ties with its home country.

Capital markets have also become more and more organized since the end of the war through institutions such as the International Monetary Fund (IMF) and the Organization of Petroleum Exporting Countries (OPEC) and through mechanisms such as the "swap arrangements" between countries. Other markets have been organized through labour unions, cartels, marketing boards, trade agreements and so on.

In parallel with the organization of markets we are witnessing attempts to form trading blocs which are seeking to become more self-sufficient. This at a time when moves are underway under General Agreement on Trade & Tariffs (GATT) to liberalize trade. Some of these trading blocs are:

- the European Economic Community (EEC) which has a larger GNP and does much more world trade than the USA. It includes Britain which is still an important trading partner for Canada;

- the Council for Mutual Economic Assistance (Comecon), which is the Soviet equivalent of the EEC;

- OPEC which has come to dominate the international oil market;

- the Association of Southeast Asian Nations (ASEAN) which has replaced the US sponsored SEATO pact;

- the Andean Pact Commission (ANCOM) which allies six South American countries;

- the Treaty of Izmir, signed in the summer of 1976, which initiated a free trade zone between Iran, Pakistan and Turkey.

The formation of regional and sectoral trading blocs has major implications for Canada, since we are one of the few industrialized countries, which does not adhere to any formal free trade bloc. Canada has not been too successful so far in attempts to diversify her international trading relationships.

b) The Emergence of the Third World and Increasing East-West Trade

The Third World's increasing political freedom since 1945 from the earlier colonial powers, has led to greater and greater emphasis on independent economic development strategies. Early strategies in the less developed countries aimed to accelerate industrialization by means of technology transfer. Direct foreign investment was often chosen as the mechanism to achieve such transfer. In recent years, however, the developing countries have begun to shy away from this approach to industrialization, because it seemed to lead to a new dependence on the more advanced countries. Moreover, the underdeveloped countries began to recognize that their populations were not necessarily better off as a result of western type industrialization. Indeed, Third World countries, as a group, have begun to press for changes—a New International Economic Order—that will redress past dependence on the industrialized world and provide real opportunities for a more equitable share of the world's wealth. The four main areas of reform are spelled out in Resolution 3362 of the Sixth Special Session of the UN in September 1975:

1. policies on commodities (pricing, stockpiling, compensatory financing);

2. policies on promoting exports of manufactures by developing countries (reduction of tariff and non-tariff barriers, adjustment assistance in developed countries, preferential access);

3. policies on international finance (preferential terms on special drawing rights (sdrs) for developing countries, recycling of petro-dollars, debt burden);

4. policies on foreign investment and technology transfer (code of behaviour for multinational firms, control of restrictive business practices, new patent convention, code of conduct for technology transfer).

Demands for such policies are on the agendas of most international meetings today and the thinking behind them is reflected in a growing number of national and regional policies (e.g. Andean Pact) that are accelerating the birth of a New International Economic Order. Third World countries already dominate world trade in more than a dozen major commodities! Cartels or commodity agreements are more and more in evidence and it is clear that many developing countries are putting politics before profits by trading at or sometimes below production costs to break into world trade.

Exports from LDCs will inevitably have adverse effects on high cost commodity export countries such as Canada. For example, as recently as 1965 Canada produced two-thirds of the world's nickel, whereas by 1975 we were providing only about one-third of the world's requirements.

However, it is the LDCs determined incursion into secondary manufacturing that is most likely to bring about long term structural changes in world trade. Import substitution behind high tariff walls was the strategy of many countries in the 1950s and 1960s, with emphasis in such sectors as textiles, shoes and clothing. More recently the focus has shifted to promoting exports of light manufactured goods (light engineering products, electrical equipment) in which LDCs generally have a comparative advantage because they can produce at low cost with labour-intensive technologies. The major markets for such goods are in developed countries, including Canada.

The countries of eastern Europe are also expanding into new markets. The annual growth rate of exports from eastern European countries to the West soared from 9.6% during the 1960/65 period to 47.2% in 1974 (21.2 billion dollars worth of exports in 1974).[8] The availability of vast reserves of raw materials in the Soviet Union constitute an important incentive for the more developed countries to trade with this block of countries e.g. the Soviet gas pipeline to Western Europe. The growing integration of the centrally-planned economies into the world economy has major implications for future economic development since the eastern Europeans will be in direct competition with Canada and other western countries for world markets, not only for resources but also for industrial products such as heavy machinery.

c) The World Today

Post-war developments have resulted in global trade flows as illustrated in Figure 3-1; a striking level of interdependence.

This interdependence clearly means that everyone is affected by the actions of any particular group. The actions of OPEC and the international debate over the Soviet gas pipeline to Europe well illustrate the situation.

Since 1973 the world has adjusted to rising oil prices. Banks in Western countries loaned some $600 billion to oil producing and other developing countries based on the assumption of continued demand for oil and constantly increasing oil prices as well as promising trade prospects. With the recent recession and the associated slowing-down of economic activity, an oil glut has resulted with a break in the OPEC dominated prices and thus many developing countries cannot repay these loans. This shock is being felt in the banking establishment around the world.

Canadian banks participated in these international transactions. For example, as highlighted in its 1982 Annual Report, the Bank of Nova Scotia reported foreign assets of $28.9 billion. Some $5.1 billion is in Latin America and the Caribbean; $4.4 billion is in loans to higher-income developing countries and $600 million in other developing countries.

The debt-ridden countries can be expected to compete ferociously for foreign markets in the 1980s to obtain foreign currency to service their debts. Canada will inevitably find herself competing in the same markets with these countries which, generally have massive labour cost advantages and often extensive government financial support. The international labour rates in the manufacturing sector, for example, illustrate the dimensions of the problem (see Table 3-1), to be faced by Canada.

The uncertainty, which has grown in the international economic system in the 1970s, and the world-wide recession with associated large-scale unemployment, has led governments to turn increasingly inward to protect their immediate interests. Despite much rhetoric to the contrary, protectionism has increased in the 1970s and international trade has increasingly been constrained. The focus of international trade has seemingly shifted from "free trade" to "fair trade." One estimate of the extent of the growth in "managed" international trade is shown in Figure 3-2.

Figure 3-1
The Arteries of Trade

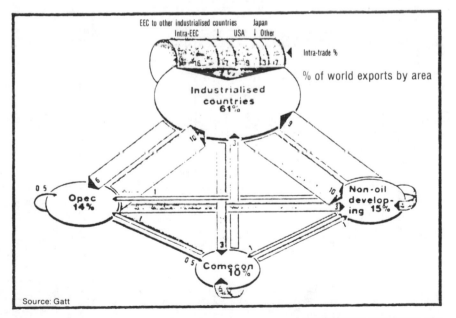

Source: Gatt

THE ECONOMIST DECEMBER 25 1982

TABLE 3-1
Estimated Hourly Compensation[1] of Production Workers in Manufacturing. Canada and Other Industrial and Newly Industrialized Countries, 1970-81

	1970	1971	1972	1973	1974	1975	1976	1977	1978	1979	1980	1981
						(U.S. dollars)						
Industrial countries:												
Canada	3.46	3.91	4.31	4.66	5.45	6.11	7.20	7.54	7.69	8.15	9.04	9.86
United States	4.18	4.49	4.84	5.26	5.75	6.35	6.93	7.59	8.30	9.08	10.00	11.06
Belgium	2.06	2.44	3.16	4.19	5.12	6.54	7.03	8.46	10.39	12.02	13.18	11.13
France	1.72	1.93	2.34	3.08	3.41	4.58	4.76	5.31	6.54	7.90	9.23	8.28
Germany	2.33	2.76	3.34	4.56	5.32	6.19	6.60	7.79	9.65	11.26	12.26	10.47
Italy	1.74	2.10	2.55	3.17	3.62	4.60	4.38	5.08	6.09	7.19	8.26	7.59
Netherlands	2.12	2.55	3.13	4.28	5.33	6.53	6.98	8.15	9.98	11.47	12.17	10.25
Sweden	2.93	3.23	4.03	4.93	5.63	7.18	8.21	8.85	9.65	11.33	12.51	11.88
United Kingdom	1.49	1.74	2.03	2.25	2.60	3.27	3.12	3.35	4.28	5.50	7.37	7.43
Japan	0.99	1.18	1.58	2.19	2.67	3.05	3.30	4.03	5.54	5.49	5.61	6.23
	1970	1971	1972	1973	1974	1975	1976	1977	1978	1979	1980	1981
Newly industrialized countries:												
Mexico	...	...	...	...	...	1.89	1.95	1.75	2.01	2.34	2.97	3.65
Brazil	...	...	...	...	...	1.13	1.29	1.46	1.67	1.73	1.70	2.14
Korea	...	...	...	...	...	0.37	0.47	0.63	0.86	1.14	1.09	1.17
Hong Kong	...	...	...	...	...	...	...	...	1.13	1.25	1.30	1.40
Taiwan	...	...	...	...	...	...	...	...	0.80	1.01	1.27	1.52

1. Total hourly compensation includes all payments made directly to the worker (pay for time worked, pay for vacations and other leave, all bonuses, and pay in kind *before* payroll deductions of any kind). It *also includes* "fringe benefits" such as employer expenditures for social security, insurance, and so on. The information is derived from periodic labour cost surveys, prorated to intervening years. Small differences in compensation levels should not be considered significant. Total compensation is computed per hour worked.

Source: U.S. Department of Labor, Bureau of Labor Statistics, Office of Productivity and Technology, July 1982 (unpublished data).

In this study Canada is shown as one of the least protectionist countries. This has been Canadian policy, of course, due to the traditional view that the country is a trading nation, exporting nearly 30% of its GDP (see Table 3-2), and thus the fewer barriers exist to trade the better.

As a result of this policy Canada, for example, does not subsidize her exports as heavily as other industrialized countries (see Figure 3-3).

With growing international interdependence in the post-war period, the US has experienced a relative loss of economic power (see Table 3-3). For example, the US share of world exports declined from 21.3% in 1970 to 17% in 1978 while it has become increasingly more dependent on imports which have grown from 3.4% of GNP in 1946 to 10.3% in 1978. Meanwhile Canada has increased its share of exports to the US from 53% of total exports in 1960 to 70% in 1980, a proportion which now equals the long-standing level of the US share of imports into Canada.

Even though Japan has become Canada's second largest trading partner after the US, it is very much open to question as to whether the continued heavy dependence of Canada on the US market is truly in the national interest, particularly since the US is in relative decline vis-à-vis the faster growing Third World markets where Canada directs only 10% of its exports.

Figure 3-2
Growth in Managed International Trade
in the 1970s

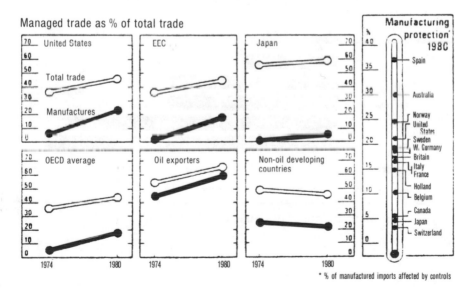

Source: Page S.: "The Management of International Trade": Discussion Paper No. 29; National Institute of Economic and Social Research, London 1982.

TABLE 3-2
Relative Exports in
Selected OECD Countries (1980)

Country	Exports as per cent of GDP
Sweden	29.8
CANADA	29.3
U.K.	28.3
West Germany	27.5
Italy	25.2
France	22.4
Japan	13.9
U.S.A.	10.1

Source: U.N. Yearbook of International Trade Statistics 1981.

Figure 3-3
Government Support of Exports

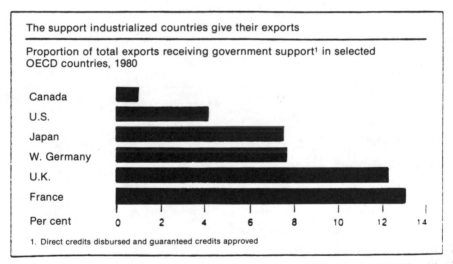

The support industrialized countries give their exports

Proportion of total exports receiving government support[1] in selected OECD countries, 1980

Canada
U.S.
Japan
W. Germany
U.K.
France

Per cent　0　2　4　6　8　10　12　14

1. Direct credits disbursed and guaranteed credits approved

Source: Economic Council of Canada; "Au Courant" Vol.3, No.3 1982 p.11.

The realignments that Canada may have to seek to achieve in the 1980s to re-establish economic health are bound to increase stresses on socio-economic institutions, on the resource base and on the environment. The importance of these stresses are examined more specifically in the following chapters.

TABLE 3-3
Relative Decline of American Power

	1950	1980
Military		
• US % of world military expenditures	50	23
• Nuclear position	US effective monopoly plus invulnerability	US-Soviet parity plus proliferation
Economic		
• US % of world GNP	34	23
• US % of world manufactured products	60	30
• US % of world monetary reserves	50	6
Political	Leading role in reconstruction of Western Europe and Japan; organizer of alliance systems	Member of multi-polar world; key ally of Japan and Western Europe

Source: Ushiba N., Allison G., DeMontbrial T.; Sharing International Responsibility; Trilateral Commission Report No. 25, 1983.

Reference
8. *Out of Joint with the Times*, op. cit., p.13.

4. Canada's Position in the New International Economic Environment

Canada's balance of international payments summarizes all economic transactions between Canada and the rest of the world. It is an important barometer of our economic relations with the world and an indicator of how well we are faring in the international environment. In addition, for a small open economy such as Canada, the balance of payments reflects the structural evolution of the economy and highlights potential future developments.

a) The Current Account

The current account summarizes four types of transactions:

1. Merchandise Trade — exports and imports of goods;

2. Services rendered to or by residents of other countries — freight, travel, business services, etc.;

3. Interest and dividends received on Canadian investments abroad and paid on foreign investment in Canada;

   and,

4. Transfers of funds that are not associated with the provision of goods and services.

When a country's total receipts from abroad under these four headings exceed total payments, it is said to have a surplus on current account. On the other hand, when total payments exceed total receipts, the country has a deficit on current account (Figure 4-1). It is then spending more than it is earning internationally and must draw on savings from abroad to make up the difference. Foreign savings coming into Canada and Canadian savings going abroad are shown in the capital account.

Canada is essentially an open, resource exporting country. Her trade balance on Merchandise has been consistently favourable over the past decade or so, as the following details display:

In contrast to the consistently favourable Merchandise Trade Balance, Canada has suffered from a chronic deficit on her international Service Payments Account, as shown below:

Figure 4-1
Canada's Current Account
Balance of Payments

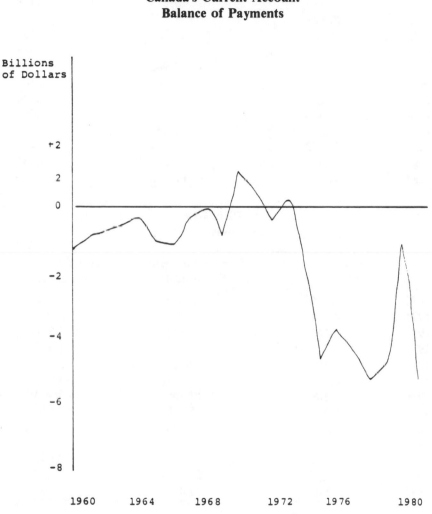

Source: Appendix I

TABLE 4-1
(Millions of $)

Years	Merchandise Exports	Merchandise Imports	Trade Balance
1970	16,921	13,869	3,052
1971	17,877	15,316	2,561
1972	20,129	18,272	1,851
1973	25,461	22,726	2,735
1974	32,591	30,902	1,689
1975	33,511	33,962	-451
1976	37,995	36,607	1,388
1977	44,253	41,523	2,730
1978	53,054	49,047	4,007
1979	65,275	61,157	4,118
1980	76,772	68,284	8,488
1981	84,221	76,870	7,351
1982	84,486	66,740	17,746

TABLE 4-1A
(Millions of $)

Years	Service Payment Receipts	Service Payments to Non-Residents	Service Payments Balance
1970	4,246	6,345	-2,099
1971	4,304	6,702	-2,398
1972	4,451	6,978	-2,527
1973	5,257	8,228	-2,971
1974	6,401	10,107	-3,706
1975	6,941	11,627	-4,686
1976	7,606	13,366	-5,760
1977	8,295	15,739	-7,444
1978	9,931	18,923	-8,992
1979	11,906	21,650	-9,744
1980	14,172	25,003	-10,831
1981	15,247	29,505	-14,258
1982	15,909	32,410	-16,501

The data below summarize the overall Balance of International Payments on Current Account for Canada over the past 13 years:

TABLE 4-1B
(Millions of $)

Years	Trade Balance (Surpluses or Deficits)	Service Payments Balance (Surpluses or Deficits)	Canadian Surpluses or Deficits on Current (Goods & Services) Accts.
1970	3,052	−2,099	953
1971	2,561	−2,398	163
1972	1,857	−2,527	−670
1973	2,735	−2,971	−236
1974	1,689	−3,706	−2,017
1975	−451	−4,686	−5,137
1976	1,388	−5,760	−4,372
1977	2,730	−7,444	−4,714
1978	4,007	−8,992	−4,985
1979	4,118	−9,744	−5,626
1980	8,488	−10,831	−2,343
1981	7,351	−14,258	−6,907
1982	17,746	−16,501	1,245

The above statistics are depicted graphically in Figure 4-2.

TABLE 4-2
Canada's Current Account Balance of International Payments
($000,000)

	1970	1972	1974	1976	1978	1980	1981	1982
Merchandise Trade	+3,052	+1,857	+1,689	+1,388	+4,007	+8,488	+7,351	+17,746
Service Transactions:								
Travel	-226	-234	-284	-1,191	-1,706	-1,228	-1,116	-1,282
Interest & Dividends	-997	-1,048	-1,553	-2,498	-4,696	-5,384	-6,474	-9,303
Freight & Shipping	+37	-74	-224	-150	+131	+536	+487	+895
Other Services	-556	-884	-1,215	-1,417	-2,111	-3,760	-6,045	-6,811
Withholding Tax	-269	-287	-430	-504	-582	-995	-1,110	-1,178
Balance on Service Transactions	-2,099	-2,527	-3,706	-5,760	-8,992	-10,831	-14,258	-16,501
Balance on Goods and Services	+953	-670	-2,017	-4,372	-4,985	-2,343	-6,907	+1,245
Net Transfers (including Withholding Tax receipts)	-115	+284	+557	+530	+50	+1,247	+1,561	+1,424
Balance on Current Account	+1,060	+386	-1,460	-3,842	-5,302	-1,096	-5,346	+2,669

Source: Bank of Canada Review, April 1983

Figure 4-2

Table 1 Merchandise Trade Balance

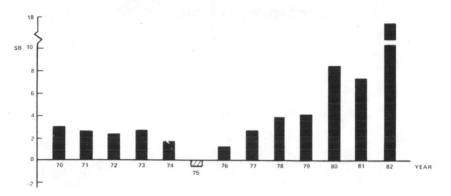

Table 2 Service Payments Balance

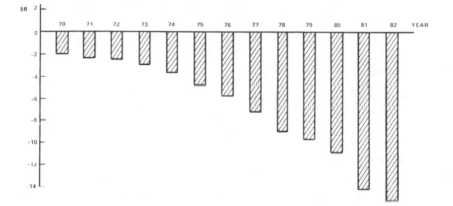

Table 3 Canadian Surpluses or Deficits on International Accounts

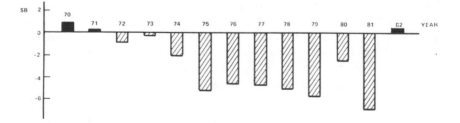

Figure 4-3
Canada's Balance of Payments
In Merchandise and Non-Merchandise
Trade Expressed as a Percent of GNP

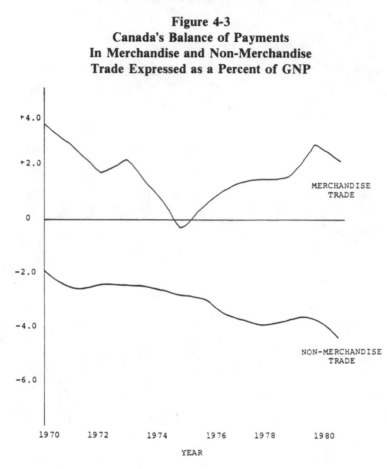

Traditionally, Canada has thus evidently relied on a surplus in her merchandise trade to balance a deficit in service transactions. However, during the last decade, Canada has clearly been unable to generate a sufficiently large merchandise trade surplus to offset a growing deficit on services (Tables 4-1, 4-2). The rather anomalous performance since 1982 was due to reduced imports brought about by recessionary conditions rather than any spectacular increases in exports and thus it is apparent that over the years the services deficit has been expanding much more rapidly than the overall economy.* Consequently, the deficit in services is now so large, and is rising at such a rate, that it is difficult to see how the trade surplus can possibly catch up with it (Figure 4-2).

---

*The current account is expected to be in its traditional deficit in 1984 due to increased imports with economic recovery.

Furthermore, while Canada's merchandise trade is highly responsive to shifts in international market conditions, the country's services deficit is structural in nature and largely due to past borrowings from abroad. Approximately one half of the deficit in "other" services and all of the outflow of dividend payments, can be attributed to remittances from Canadian subsidiaries to their parent firms abroad. The level of interest payments flowing out of Canada in turn is a reflection of past borrowings from abroad that usually entail fixed long term commitments. In consequence, neither of these service payments is responsive to short run palliatives. Indeed, it is clearly apparent that Canada's overall deficit in service transactions can only be corrected over a very long time without placing intolerable pressures on the value of the Canadian dollar in international money markets.

b) The Capital Account

The transactions that Canada has traditionally employed to finance its current account deficits and to add to its foreign assets or liabilities are recorded in the capital account of the balance of payments (Table 4-3).

Capital movements are divided into long-term (more than one year) and short-term flows (less than one year) according to the expected duration of the investment. Long-term and short-term capital movements together produce a net inflow or outflow of capital. The net flow may be equal to, exceed, or fall short of the deficit on current account. Apart from errors and omissions, differences between the balance on current account and on capital account will result in either an increase or a decrease in a country's foreign exchange reserves.

Historically, Canada has relied on a net inflow of investment capital (direct and portfolio) to finance its current account deficits and to augment foreign exchange reserves. This inflow of foreign capital has allowed and indeed encouraged Canada to consume more than it produced for many years. The interest and dividend payments, associated with these past inflows of long-term capital, are however primarily responsible for the continuing current account deficit. Moreover, during the 1970s the structure of this capital movement shifted in an unfavourable manner. Since 1974, the tradi tional net inflow of direct investment into Canada has been replaced by an increasingly large net outflow of direct investment capital with the result that we have become much more dependent on large inflows of portfolio investment and short term borrowings from abroad to finance our current consumption. Canada's heavy reliance on this type of borrowing in recent years will place an increasing stress on current account in the future, since it entails fixed term commitments that must be honoured annually irrespective of the health of the domestic economy. Furthermore, while these recent infusions of debt capital have allowed Canada to temporarily postpone a fundamental restructuring of its international payments, the added pressures that these borrowings will place in future on the current account, virtually ensure that such a restructuring must occur before very long.

TABLE 4-3
Canada's Balance of Payments on Capital Account
($000,000)

	1970	1972	1974	1976	1978	1980	1981	1982
Capital Account Balance:								
Direct Investment	+590	+220	+35	-890	-2135	-2565	-10500	-1225
Portfolio Trans.	+563	+1596	+1772	+8654	+5081	+5035	+10531	+11279
Other Long-Term Capital Movements	-146	-228	-766	+159	+333	-1563	+527	-1493
Balance on Long-Term Capital Movements	+1007	+1588	+1041	+7923	+3279	+907	+558	+8561
Balance on Short-Term Capital Movements	-196	+472	+1310	+99	+461	-730	+15072	-9411
Net Capital Movements	+811	+2060	+2351	+8022	+3740	+177	+15630	-850
Total Current and Capital Account Balance	+1871	+1674	+891	+4180	-1562	-919	+10284	+1819
Net Errors and Omissions	-387	-1455	-867	-3658	-1737	-578	-9068	-2514
Allocation of SDRs	+133	+117	—	—	—	+217	+210	—
Net Official Monetary Movements	+1617	+336	+24	+522	-3299	-1280	+1426	-695

Source: Appendix I

In fact, Canada only narrowly averted a major balance of payments crisis in 1981 as a result of the National Energy Program. Motivated by policies that encouraged Canadian ownership of companies in the oil and gas sector, Canadians acquired, on a large scale, the domestic assets owned by non-resident direct investors. These acquisitions were largely financed by bank borrowings. In order to finance this surge of lending, Canada's chartered banks borrowed more than $20.0 billion in international money markets through their foreign subsidiaries on a short term basis. As a result, the foreign currency liabilities of Canada's chartered banks to non-residents increased by almost $16.5 billion in 1981. However, despite this large capital inflow, as the pace of acquisitions increased, the external value of the dollar was pushed to record lows. This forced the Minister of Finance to intervene and request that the chartered banks limit the amount of lending to residents for use in the financing of takeovers. It is now abundantly clear that if the Minister of Finance had not intervened, or if the chartered banks had not borrowed such large sums internationally, Canada would have faced a major balance of payments crisis. As it is, the problem may have merely been postponed, rather than averted, since Canada's chartered banks must eventually repay the international loans.

Nevertheless, the recent adverse changes in the capital account are not responsible for the difficulties that the Canadian dollar has experienced since 1977. The real cause of the problem is rooted in the current account deficit. If the current account was in balance, short run changes in the capital account would be of little consequence. As already indicated, however, the problem in the current account stems from an inadequate merchandise trade surplus to offset the ever increasing outflow of service payments due to some extent at least to the large investment of foreign capital in Canada. Interest payments in particular have increased in recent years, due not only to large borrowings, but also to higher interest rates and the depreciation of the Canadian dollar on international money markets. This increase in payment will continue unabated, until the current account deficit, which makes these borrowings necessary, is somehow corrected.

c) Canada's Merchandise Trade

The consensus among economic analysts is that Canada's current account deficit can only be corrected through a large and sustained increase in our merchandise trade surplus. An increase in the merchandise surplus would reduce or eliminate the need for further inflows of long term capital, and thus break the cycle of debt servicing payments that have crippled the Canadian dollar.[9] It is therefore necessary to examine the structure of Canada's merchandise trade in greater detail in order to identify areas of present and potential future strength that could be utilized to generate a substantial increase in net exports from Canada.

TABLE 4-4
Canada's Commodity Trade*
($000,000)

	1960	1965	1970	1975	1980	1981	1982
Agricultural Products							
Exports	988.0	1708.9	1868.5	4062.6	8214.8	9404.8	10219.7
Imports	582.3	769.7	1115.5	2694.8	4802.8	5181.1	4939.3
Balance	+405.7	+939.2	+753.0	+1367.8	+3412.0	+4223.7	+5280.4
Crude Materials							
Exports	1114.5	1763.7	3068.2	7953.6	14756.2	15168.1	14760.4
Imports	745.2	1006.3	1171.8	5078.1	11335.4	12150.0	8672.9
Balance	+369.3	+757.4	+1896.4	+2875.5	+3420.8	+3018.1	+6087.5
Fabricated Materials							
Exports	2727.9	3728.8	5866.4	9796.0	29333.9	30534.6	27,883.0
Imports	1334.9	2114.4	2885.4	5953.8	12700.7	14529.0	11,794.4
Balance	+1393.0	+1614.4	+2981.0	+3842.2	+16633.2	+16005.6	+16,088.6
End Products							
Exports	411.2	1300.1	5566.8	10097.3	21726.3	25129.0	28,336.9
Imports	2726.4	4476.3	8617.7	20610.1	39525.6	45801.5	40,932.9
Balance	-2315.2	-3176.2	-3050.9	-10,512.8	-17799.3	-20672.5	-12596.0
Total Commodity Trade							
Exports	5255.6	8525.1	16401.1	31995.7	74259.3	80895.2	81464.0
Imports	5482.7	8633.1	13951.9	34667.6	69127.6	78665.0	67355.3
Balance	-227.1	-108.0	+2449.2	-2671.9	+5131.7	+2230.2	+14,108.7

*Customs Valuation Basis
Source: Appendix II

As Table 4-4 and Figure 4-4 clearly indicate, Canada has traditionally relied on the export of a basket of crude and semi-processed resource staples to finance its appetite for imported manufactured products and to generate a merchandise trade surplus. Canada's commodity exports and imports can be divided into four main categories, viz agricultural products (meat, grains, etc.); crude raw materials (minerals & hydrocarbons); fabricated materials (lumber, newsprint, semi-processed metals, etc.); and manufactured end products (electrical products, machinery, transportation equipment, etc.).

Figure 4-4
Canada's Commodity Trade Balance

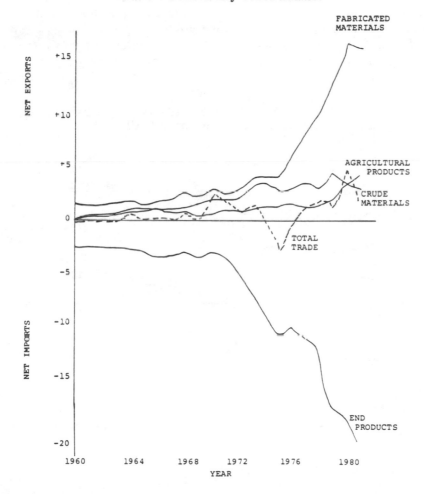

Source: Appendix II

Historically, Canada has experienced a relatively large and increasing trade surplus in agricultural products and crude and fabricated materials, but a massive trade deficit in finished end products. Generally, the surplus generated by the former has been more than adequate to offset our large deficit in the latter. However, the base of this trade surplus is extremely narrow and has not changed significantly in the last twenty years. For example, in 1980, exports of meat, fish and cereals accounted for almost 80 percent of Canada's food and agricultural exports, while shipments of iron, copper, and nickel ores and concentrates, combined with crude petroleum products represented some 70 percent of our exports of crude materials. Exports of fabricated materials, which have become relatively more important during the last decade, are also dominated by the shipments of a few resource-based industries, such as wood products, primary chemicals, and metals. In 1980, these industries accounted for two-thirds of Canada's exports of fabricated materials. Moreover, as the Canadian economy expands, we

Figure 4-5
Canada's Commodity Trade Balance
Expressed as a Percent of GNP

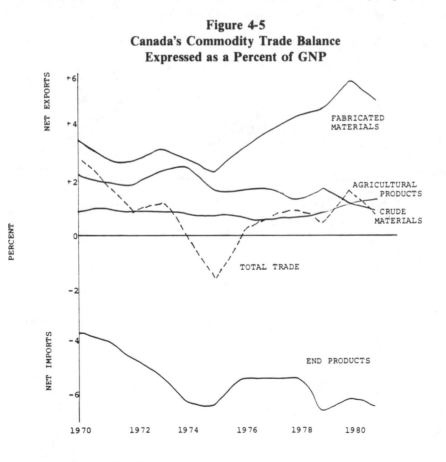

Source: Appendix II.

seem to be becoming more and more dependent upon these resource-based commodities to offset our ever-increasing trade deficit in manufactured end products (see Figure 4-5).

A similar picture emerges when Canada's total trade in manufactured goods (fabricated materials + end products) is examined in relation to the level of technological intensity inherent in these products. Figure 4-6 summarizes the trade performance of industries with high, medium, low and no research and development expenditures.[10] As this chart indicates, Canada has experienced an increasingly large deficit in high technology manufactures trade during the last decade. In contrast, industries that are of medium research-intensity have achieved a growing trade surplus. Industries that carry out no R&D whatsoever have also experienced a steady deterioration in their trade performance during this period, while low research-intensive industries have managed to generate a moderate trade surplus since 1976.

Figure 4-6
Canada's Trade Balance in Manufactured Products
by Research Intensity

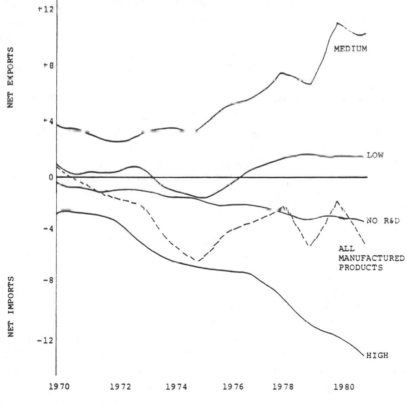

Source: Appendix III.

However, the rapid rise in the trade surplus of industries with a medium research intensity is entirely a reflection of Canada's comparative advantage in resource-based products and seems totally unrelated to the successful application of even moderately sophisticated technologies. Within this group, paper and allied products, primary metals and petroleum and coal industries account for over 95 percent of the trade surplus generated annually.[11] In addition, the deteriorating trade performance of our high technology industries suggests that Canada faces a significant relative disadvantage in the manufacture and export of these products and that the absolute magnitude of this disadvantage is increasing. In 1981, Canada's deficit in high technology manufactures trade exceeded $12.0 billion. In fact, the disappointing trade performance of this sector is found to be largely responsible for the massive deficit in end products trade that Canada has experienced in recent years.

This analysis suggests that Canada's relative advantage in international markets remains firmly rooted in the extraction and export of semi-processed and processed resource-based commodities and that Canada is at a significant disadvantage in the manufacture and export of high technology products. It also appears that there are really only two options available for increasing Canada's merchandise trade surplus and thus reducing the deficit on our current account. One option would involve a substantial increase in Canada's trade surplus in primary and resource based-products, whereas the second alternative would call for a significant reduction in the deficit in end products trade through an increase in net exports of technology-intensive manufactures. However, even if both of these alternatives were vigorously pursued, it is considered totally unrealistic to expect a reversal in Canada's trade deficit in high technology manufactures in the short or medium term, given the magnitude of the relative disadvantage that Canada seems to face. Canada currently does not possess the manufacturing capability or the technological expertise to produce most of the high technology products that are presently imported. Effort designed to put such capability and expertise in place would require a very significant investment of resources over a prolonged period of time before any tangible results emerged. In fact, even if all governments in Canada adopted a vigorous industrial strategy today that emphasized high technology industries, it would be at least a decade before such a strategy yielded significant returns.

Unfortunately, Canada's international balance of payments difficulties need to be redressed rather expeditiously in order to reverse Canada's current account deficit and thus lessen the country's dependence on inflows of capital from abroad. For every year of delay, the claims of non-residents on Canada's economy will increase, with the resulting debt servicing payments multiplying in size. As ex-Department of Finance senior official A.F.W. Plumptree concluded in his analysis of the Canadian economy:

"The basic threat to Canadian economic independence . . . lies in a continuing balance of payments deficit that has to be covered by capital imports which are at any time subject to interruption and which involve increasing impairment of Canadian control over the economy."[12]

The primary alternative open to Canada in the medium term appears to be to generate a significantly larger merchandise trade surplus through the accelerated exploitation and export of resource based products. In its Seventeenth Annual Review (1980), the Economic Council of Canada recommended that increased exports of natural gas, electricity and coal should be utilized to the fullest extent possible in order to reduce Canada's current account deficit.[13] In making this recommendation, the Council emphasized that the output of the planned larger energy projects was urgently required to help in the resolution of the international payments problem and warned that any delay in these projects could result in an increase, rather than a reduction, in the need for foreign capital in Canada over the medium and long term. The large amounts of foreign capital imported by Canada in 1981 and 1982 suggests that the Economic Council's conclusion may in fact prove to have been correct.

d) Trade and Stresses in the Future

Achieving a significant increase in Canada's traditional resource-based exports will not be easy during the next decade. International commodity markets are almost certain to be more competitive and volatile in the future than they have been in the past, due to the massive debt load of many of the world's principal suppliers of primary products (Table 4-5). In addition, many of the world's largest debtor nations would seem to have a relative advantage in exactly the same primary commodities that Canada can offer. These heavily indebted countries will be forced to seek an expansion in their exports of primary products in the future, regardless of international market conditions, in order to earn the foreign exchange required to service their massive debts. For example, Brazil, the world's largest debtor nation, is highly dependent upon exports of primary minerals and coffee as a source of foreign exchange. Since payments on its international debt now exceed 117 percent of the country's export earnings, Brazil has little choice other than to dump ever increasing quantities of these commodities on international markets in order to secure the foreign exchange required to repay its debts. Mexico and Venezuela are in exactly the same position with respect to crude petroleum and petroleum products. Shipments of petroleum and natural gas represent over two-thirds of Mexico's exports and account for almost 90 percent of Venezuela's export earnings. Exports of agricultural products such as meat and cereals (wheat) are Argentina's principal source of foreign exchange and account for over one-third of the country's total export earnings. In order to avoid defaulting on its debt service payments, Argentina must drastically increase the production and export of these commodities in the future. In

1983, the interest and principal due on Argentina's international debt have exceeded 150 percent of the country's export earnings in 1982. Zaire, Zambia and the Philippines are also entangled in a similar debt trap and have no alternative other than to export more of their wealth in primary minerals (iron ore, copper, nickel) to meet their international obligations.

TABLE 4-5
Estimated International Debt of Selected Nations
(Billions of U.S. $)

	Total at Year End—1982	Debt Service Payment—1983*	Payment as a % of Exports
Brazil	87.0	30.8	117%
Mexico	80.1	43.1	126%
Argentina	43.0	18.4	153%
South Korea	36.0	15.7	49%
Venezuela	28.0	19.9	101%
Israel	26.7	15.2	126%
Poland	26.0	7.8	94%
U.S.S.R.	23.0	12.2	25%
Egypt	19.2	6.0	46%
Yugoslavia	19.0	6.0	41%
Philippines	16.6	7.0	79%
East Germany	14.0	6.3	83%
Peru	11.5	3.9	79%
Rumania	9.9	5.5	61%
Nigeria	9.3	4.9	28%
Hungary	7.0	3.5	55%
Zaire	5.1	1.2	83%
Zambia	4.5	2.0	195%
Bolivia	3.1	1.0	118%

*Includes interest and amortization due on debt in 1983
Source: Morgan Guaranty Trust Company

Further heavy emphasis upon resource development in Canada will place increasing stress upon the country's land, water, air, forest, fish, etc. endowment and on the total environmental system. Canada is said to have already reached the upper limit of good land available for agricultural development and further expansion of cultivated acreage will require the exploitation of land with inherently lower productivity. The total land area presently under cultivation in Canada amounts to some 69 million hectares. While an additional 60 million hectares have the potential for additional crop production, most of this reserve lies in northern regions and is subject to less favourable soil and climatic conditions. Bringing this land into commercial production will require the development of new crop strains suited to the short, cool growing season that generally characterizes these regions.

It is by no means certain that Canada will be able to increase, or even maintain the productive potential of existing farm land without causing serious damage to the environment. In the last twenty years, increases in agricultural output were largely achieved through the application of ever increasing amounts of chemical herbicides, fertilizers, and pesticides to Canada's agricultural resource base. While this practice has allowed farmers to engage in monocultural and continuous production without experiencing any reduction in yields or crop quality, the persistence of these chemical residues in agricultural soils has resulted in many undesirable side effects that could seriously constrain Canada's ability to sustain agricultural production at current levels if corrective action is not taken. This progressive degradation of agricultural land appears to be most pervasive in the Prairie region. Almost one-third of the existing nitrogen in Prairie soils has been used up in crop production and can only be replaced by natural nitrogen fixation processes. In addition, up to 50% of the organic matter in some Prairie soils has been destroyed through over tillage and the excessive application of chemical additives. [14] However, soil salinity appears to be the most pressing problem facing Prairie farmers and presently affects 10% of agricultural land in the Prairies. This excessive accumulation of saline substances and salt in Prairie soils is largely due to the widespread practice of summer fallowing agricultural land in the west rather than engaging in crop rotation. Summer fallowing appears to retard the natural movement of water within the soil and accentuates the breakdown of organic matter.

The degradation of prime agricultural land is also rapidly becoming a significant problem in central Canada. Excessive reliance on chemical additives combined with the practice of monoculture in some regions have seriously depleted the organic matter in soils and rendered row crops particularly susceptible to water erosion. The annual loss of agricultural land due to sheet and rill erosion now amounts to some 13,000 acres in Ontario alone. However, a more pressing threat to prime crop land in central Canada appears to be the ever extending urban environment. As a result of urban sprawl, some 200,000 acres of agricultural land was taken out of production in Ontario between 1966-1971. Moreover, there is a continuing threat to food production in the future, since 60% of Canada's best agricultural land is located within 60 kilometres or so of major urban centres.

Evidence is also mounting that Canada's timber reserves, within economic reach, will not be adequate to allow for the future expansion of the forestry products sector on a competitive basis, unless significant improvements occur in the level of forestry management currently in effect. It would appear that Canada's forest resources have not been adequately maintained to provide a truly sustainable yield, so that in consequence, Canada will experience shortages of merchantable timber within the next decade or so unless remedial actions are taken. [15] The current situation is largely due to the overcutting of forests, accompanied by an inadequate commitment to forest renewal. While Canada's existing total timber reserves appear more than adequate to sustain the current level of harvest indefinitely, much of the remaining stock is generally located in more remote areas that lack the infrastructure required for harvesting or is stocked with less attractive grades and species that would be unprofitable to harvest. When this high cost and presently uneconomic timber is excluded from the overall inventory, it appears that Canada's timber reserves, within economic reach, are insufficient to sustain even the current level of harvest in the longer term and indeed totally inadequate to provide the basis for any future expansion of the forestry products sector. This situation can be improved however, at least to some extent, if Canada not only implements a systematic program of forest renewal, but also ensures that the resources yield their proper economic returns. This would involve abandonment of current forest utilization practices in favour of a regime of more intensive resource husbandry in areas that possess favourable soil, water, climatic and other conditions.

Any attempt to enhance the output and export sales of Canada's commercial fisheries is also subject to the constraints encountered because of natural resource limitations and international competitiveness. A recent study of the West Coast fishery concluded that Canada's salmon stocks, by far the industry's most valuable resource, are now seriously depleted as a result of past over-fishing.[16] Canada's Pacific fishing industry is also plagued with chronic excess production capacity and a grossly overexpanded fishing fleet that have depressed the economic returns available to all participants in the industry. Moreover, it appears that these problems are a direct result of past shortcomings in fisheries management, combined with the granting of far too many commercial fishing licences—Canada's Atlantic fishery is also claimed to suffer because of inefficiency, and problems due to overcapacity. The major difficulty facing the East Coast fishery is however not inadequate stocks, but rather the absence of suitable markets for the industry's output. The often outmoded harvesting and processing techniques, still employed by the Atlantic fishery, frequently result in a low quality product that is extremely difficult to sell in the highly competitive international market at other than a distress price.

Accelerating the development of Canada's mineral and energy resources would also place an unprecedented degree of stress on the environment, e.g. mineral exploration, which requires access to large tracts of land, often conflicts with efforts to shield wilderness areas from commercial development. Once a mineral deposit is discovered, mining, particularly open pit mining, can inflict serious damage upon the immediate environment and also have a detrimental effect on water quality. In addition, current mineral processing activities often adversely affect air and water quality by dispersing various substances into the atmosphere and through leaching. Acid rain, caused by the emission of sulphur dioxide and nitrogen oxides into the air is probably the most serious environmental problem facing Canada today. One of the major sources of these emissions comprise non-ferrous metal smelters, which presently account for over 40% of the sulphur dioxide emissions in Eastern Canada.[17] While the technology exists to reduce significantly these emissions, problems remain concerning the funding of the extensive pollution abatement equipment required. Until this issue is resolved and unless the level of contaminants emitted by metal smelters is reduced, it appears socially unacceptable to stimulate the further expansion of the Canadian minerals sector.

The further development of Canada's energy resources also poses significant problems. Production from conventional oil and gas reserves in Western Canada must be expected to decline substantially over the next decade or two. Discoveries of new conventional reserves in this region of sufficient magnitude to offset this decline are considered unlikely. Indeed it would now appear that most of Canada's remaining conventional reserves may be centred in frontier regions, such as the Arctic Islands, the Beaufort Sea-Mackenzie Delta region and off the East Coast. However, the natural environment in these regions is hostile and fragile. While current, relatively limited, frontier exploration activities pose some threat to the environment, the full scale development of the resources, utilizing conventional technologies, could prove extremely hazardous. In consequence, new production technologies will have to be *developed* and *proven*, before the exploitation of Canada's frontier energy resources can proceed on a safe, economic and environmentally sound basis.

e) Canada's International Economic Relations

Canada's traditional role as a supplier of primary products to the rest of the world, mainly industrialized nations and as a large net importer of finished manufactures also affects the way in which other trading partners regard this country.

Canada is perceived as a resource hinterland by other countries. This attitude is particularly prevalent in the United States, Canada's largest trading partner. The US regards Canada as a secure source of raw materials to feed US industry and at the same time, sees Canada as a readily accessible market for the resulting manufactured products. Indeed, any attempt by Canada to alter this relationship is generally met with hostility from the U.S.A.

This attitude towards Canada is perhaps best illustrated by the reaction of the United States to Canada's National Energy Program (NEP). Attempts by the Government of Canada in 1981 to foster increased Canadian ownership of the oil and gas industry, encountered serious protests from both the US Government and the powerful American business lobby. The 25% ownership provision reserved for the Crown on every development right on Crown lands, combined with the proposed regime of exploration grants in favour of

Canadian firms were criticized by the Americans. The US Administration regarded these provisions as unwarranted interference with the right of US corporations to invest in Canada's resources and to develop them in a manner commensurate with their priorities. The NEP was perceived as an attempt to reduce the entitlement of American corporations to depletion allowances and thus reduce their income stream, lessen their capacity to borrow, depreciate their asset value and make them more susceptible to takeover by Canadian firms, which would now receive the vast majority of government incentive payments.[18] These developments would also force American firms to sell their holdings at "distress prices," since the value of the assets was being eroded, thus reducing US access to Canada's energy resources over the long term.

The United States also regarded plans to hold Canadian energy prices below world levels as an attempt by Canada to subsidize its energy intensive manufacturing industries and thus erode the competitive advantage of US industry over its relatively weaker Canadian counterpart. Countervailing action in this matter was presaged. Under pressure from the US, Canada modified some of the more contentious provisions of the NEP and publicly disavowed any intentions to extend NEP-style policies to other sectors of the economy. Plans to strengthen the Foreign Investment Review Agency were also toned down in the face of US pressures.[19] If the Canadian government had followed through with these initiatives, Canada's future economic development would have been altered in a way that appeared fundamentally inimical to traditional US interests.

A similar orientation towards Canada can also be noted in Japan, our second largest trading partner. While the Japanese are eager customers for Canadian exports of coal, natural gas and wood pulp, they have erected severe tariff and non-tariff trade barriers against Canadian exports of manufactured forestry products such as soft wood lumber and newsprint.

This view of Canada as a resource hinterland is also reflected in Japan's steadfast refusal to incorporate any Canadian content into its shipments of automotive products to Canada, despite the ever increasing penetration of Japanese motor cars in the Canadian market.

Tensions between Canada and its major trading partners can be expected to deepen as we try to restructure our economy to become more self-reliant. For example, Canada's resource hinterland image could lead to increasing pressures from the US to obtain Canadian water for the parched US mid-west.[20] Water diversion schemes would inevitably entail large scale environmental and social consequences. However, with the growing pressure to treat fresh water as a market commodity, Canada could find that it would be to its advantage to export water like other resources to strengthen its balance of payments position. Such action would be in keeping with the accepted view of Canada's role in the international economy.

References

9. For a further elaboration of this argument see H. Lukin Robinson, *Canada's Crippled Dollar*, Canadian Institute for Economic Policy, Ottawa, 1980.
10. Industries judged to be highly research-intensive include chemicals, machinery, electrical products, aircraft and parts, and scientific and professional equipment. Medium research-intensive industries include paper and allied products, primary metals, other transportation equipment, and petroleum and coal products. Industries with a low research intensity include food and beverages, tobacco, rubber and plastics, textiles, wood products, furniture and fixtures, metal fabricating, and non-metallic minerals. The industries that perform no research and development include leather, knitting mills, clothing, printing and publishing, and other miscellaneous manufacturing industries.
11. Science Council of Canada, *Hard Times, Hard Choices*, a Statement by the Science Council Industrial Policies Committee, Supply and Services Canada, November 1981, p.38.
12. Plumptree, A.F.W.: "Three Decades of Decision; Canada and the World Monetary System 1944-75," McClelland and Stewart, 1977, p.231.
13. Economic Council of Canada, *A Climate of Uncertainty*, Seventeenth Annual Review, Supply and Services Canada, 1980, p.128.
14. Agriculture Canada, *Challenge for Growth: An Agri-Food Strategy for Canada*, Ottawa, July 1981.
15. For example, see John Roberts, Minister of Environment, *A Forestry Sector Strategy for Canada*, Cabinet Discussion Paper, Ottawa, September 1981.
16. Canada, Commission on Pacific Fisheries Policy, *Turning the Tide: A New Policy for Canada's Pacific Fisheries*, Supply and Services Canada, Vancouver, September 1982, pp.13-17.
17. Energy, Mines and Resources Canada, *Mineral Policy: A Discussion Paper*, Supply and Services Canada, Ottawa, December 1981, p.100.
18. Stephen Clarkson, *Canada and the Reagan Challenge*, Canadian Institute for Economic Policy, Ottawa, 1982, p.76.
19. Clarkson, op. cit.
20. Foster H.D. and Sewell, D.: *Water — The Emerging Crisis in Canada*, Canadian Institute for Economic Policy, 1981.

5. Sectoral Perspectives

When viewed from a traditional perspective, the Canadian economy appears mature and industrially advanced. According to most conventional measures of aggregate economic performance, it also appears that the Canadian economy has done remarkably well during the last twenty years in relation to the performance of other advanced industrial nations. Over the last two decades, real domestic product has expanded at an average annual rate in excess of 7.0%, and domestic employment has increased by 3.5% annually (Table 5-1). Some rather significant shifts in the distribution of output and employment have also occurred during this period. The Canadian resource sector has experienced progressively lower rates of growth in both output and employment, while output in the manufacturing sector has increased by more than 7.5 percent per annum in real terms. In addition, like most other advanced industrialized nations, the service sector in Canada has expanded much more rapidly than the rest of the domestic economy and now accounts for the predominant proportion of economic activity (Figure 5-1).

However, while these broad economic trends suggest that there has been a significant shift in economic activity in Canada, away from the resource sector and towards more mature forms of economic activity in the manufacturing and service sectors, in reality this shift has been much less pronounced than is generally believed. In fact, the decline of the resource sector in relation to manufacturing and services (Figure 5-2) is often over-emphasized, due to the lack of adequate differentiation in published statistics between primary and secondary manufacturing activity. Primary manufacturing, such as the processing of agricultural products into foodstuffs and the conversion of logs into lumber and wood pulp, is really little more than an extension of resource harvesting activities into the processing sector.[21] Moreover, these activities are totally linked to the resource base and show little if any of the characteristics of secondary manufacturing industries, which are principally concerned with the conversion of material and labour inputs into *finished products.*

If primary processing activity is treated merely as an extension of the resource sector rather than as a part of the manufacturing sector, a very different picture of the Canadian economy emerges (Table 5-2 and Figure 5-3). While it is apparent that the overall share of real output accounted for by resource-based industry has declined since 1960, resource related activities still dominate the goods producing sector. In addition, it appears that the production of finished goods continues to play a relatively modest role in the Canadian economy and that the share of real output, originating in the

41

secondary sector, has remained almost constant during this period. *In fact, the only significant shift that has occurred in the Canadian economy has been a gradual movement away from resource related activities and towards the provision of services.*

TABLE 5-1
Real Domestic Product by Canadian Industry
1960 = 100.0

	Resources	Manufacturing	Services	Total
1960	100.0	100.0	100.0	100.0
1961	94.4	104.0	103.4	101.9
1962	107.0	113.6	108.8	109.2
1963	115.4	121.2	114.1	115.2
1964	114.6	132.9	122.0	123.0
1965	119.7	144.9	129.9	132.1
1966	130.1	155.8	137.7	140.9
1967	123.4	160.4	145.7	145.9
1968	132.9	170.4	153.2	154.1
1969	137.6	183.2	162.6	163.5
1970	145.3	180.7	168.9	167.4
1971	152.3	141.2	178.9	177.3
1972	149.3	206.0	190.4	187.7
1973	165.4	227.7	203.7	202.3
1974	157.5	235.9	216.1	211.6
1975	154.0	222.1	223.5	213.5
1976	161.1	235.3	234.3	224.1
1977	167.2	240.0	242.9	230.7
1978	159.6	252.4	252.8	238.4
1979	159.2	267.4	261.6	247.3
1980	166.9	259.5	266.4	249.3
1981	169.9	264.9	274.5	256.7
1982	158.9	231.6	272.7	246.0
Average Annual Rate of Growth				
	2.7%	6.0%	7.8%	6.6%

Source: Appendix IV

Figure 5-1
Canada
Distribution of Employment By Industry

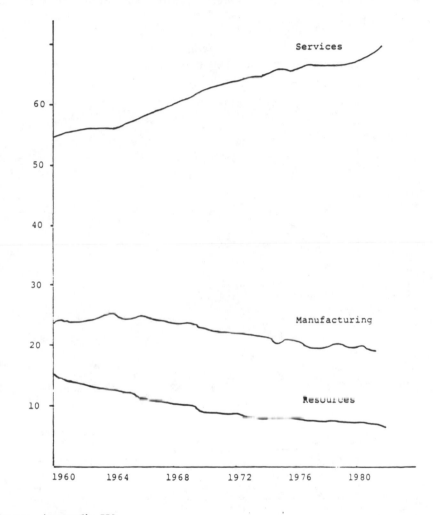

Source: Appendix IV

a) The Manufacturing Sector

The 1960-1974 period is often referred to as the "golden era" of Canadian manufacturing. This was a period of substantial and sustained real economic growth in the Canadian manufacturing sector. From 1960-1974, real output expanded at an average annual rate of 9.1% and employment in the manufacturing sector increased by 559,000 or 39.5%. Moreover, despite buoyant world

Figure 5-2
Canada
Distribution of Real Domestic Product By Industry

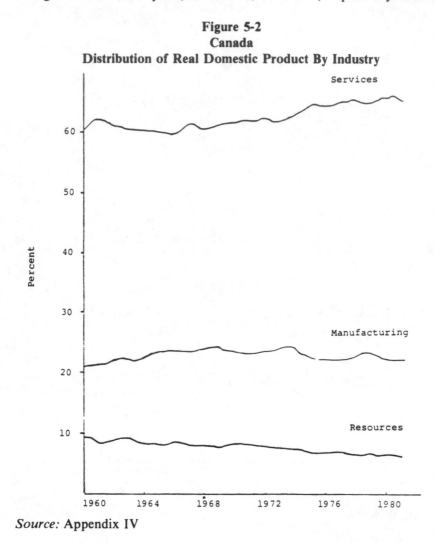

Source: Appendix IV

markets for Canadian exports of primary manufactured products, the secondary sector led this expansion. From 1960-1974, real output in the secondary sector increased by more than 11.0% per annum. The industries that expanded most rapidly during this period were rubber and plastics, machinery, electrical products, metal fabricating, transportation equipment, furniture and fixtures, as well as chemical products. Significant increases in output and employment also occurred in the primary metals, paper and allied products, as well as wood products industries.[22]

TABLE 5-2
Distribution of Real Domestic Product by Revised Industry Group

	Resource Based Industry %	Secondary Manufacturing %	Services %
1960	19.4	11.1	61.6
1961	18.9	11.3	62.5
1962	19.4	11.8	61.3
1963	19.5	12.1	61.0
1964	19.1	12.5	61.1
1965	18.7	13.0	60.6
1966	18.7	13.3	60.1
1967	17.7	13.4	61.5
1968	17.8	13.6	61.2
1969	17.5	14.0	61.3
1970	17.7	13.2	62.1
1971	17.5	13.4	62.1
1972	16.9	13.8	62.5
1973	17.1	14.4	62.0
1974	16.2	14.4	62.9
1975	15.1	13.6	64.5
1976	15.3	13.7	64.4
1977	15.3	13.5	64.9
1978	14.9	13.8	65.3
1979	14.6	14.3	65.1
1980	14.8	13.5	65.8
1981	14.5	13.6	65.9
1982	13.7	12.3	68.3

Source: Appendix IV

Figure 5-3
Canada
Distribution of Real Domestic Product
By Revised Industry Group

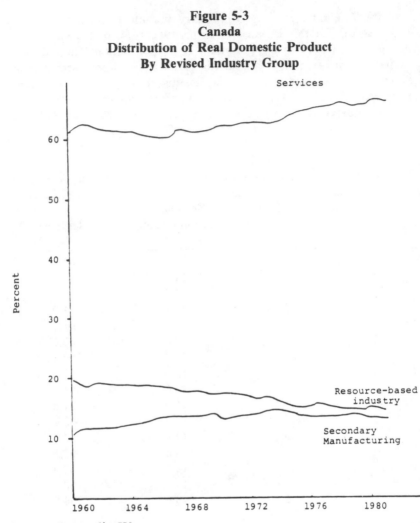

Source: Appendix IV

However, since the 1974-75 world economic recession, growth in the manufacturing sector has been slow. During this period, real growth in the Canadian manufacturing sector has averaged only 2.7% per annum, with employment having increased merely at an average annual rate of less than 2.0%. While cyclical factors have been responsible in part for the loss in economic momentum, other factors have also contributed to the sluggish progress.

Most conventional economists have been quick to point out that the rapid appreciation of the Canadian dollar in the early 1970s, combined wih the relative escalation of Canadian labour costs, have been largely responsible for the decline of the manufacturing sector. The Canadian government having abandoned in 1970 its attempt to hold the dollar at .925 (US), and having set the rate free to float. The Canadian dollar had risen to 1.04 (US), by the spring of 1974, which represented a loss in the international competitiveness of Canadian industry of approximately 12%.[23] In addition, the more rapid acceleration of wage rates in Canada from 1974-76, in relation to the labour costs of our major competitors, also served to weaken the international competitiveness of the manufacturing sector. However, while these short run factors undoubtedly contributed to the declining rate of growth experienced in the manufacturing sector during the mid-1970s, the fall in the external value of the Canadian dollar in 1977-78, combined with the moderation in domestic labour rates that has occurred since 1976, have now offset the excesses of the past. In fact, by the end of 1978, the international competitiveness of the Canadian manufacturing sector in relation to US industry had been fully restored.[24] Yet, despite these favourable conditions, the Canadian manufacturing sector continues to languish.

The drastic changes in the automotive industry have also contributed to the declining growth experienced by the manufacturing sector in recent years. During the 1960s, automotive products constituted the fastest growing segment of Canadian exports. The share of total foreign shipments accounted for by the automotive sector peaked at about 22% in the early 1970s, compared to less than 2% at the beginning of the 1960s. The stimulus for this trade explosion was, of course, the Canada-US auto pact of 1965, which provided for a rationalization of the Canadian automotive industry and its integration with US production. Under the aegis of the auto pact, real output in the Canadian automotive industry increased by about 20% per annum over the 1965-1974 decade. During this period, the auto industry's share of real output in the secondary sector also rose from an initial 11.2% to a peak of 18.0% in the early 1970s. However, since 1974, real growth in the automotive sector has faltered, leading to a reduction in both output and employment.[25] Moreover, from the mid-1970s onwards there was a net outflow of capital from Canada, reflecting disinvestment in the automotive sector, as shown in Table 5-3.

It appears that the decline in the Canadian automotive industry will accelerate during the 1980s. In a recent study, it is forcefully demonstrated that the Canadian auto industry has little, if any chance of ever matching the cost competitiveness of Japanese vehicle producers. The report estimates that Japanese auto makers presently enjoy a unit cost advantage of almost $1200 over their Canadian counterparts and that in terms of direct labour costs, Japan's advantage exceeds $1800 per unit.[26] Thus, according to the author, Canadian auto makers would have to reduce their total wage costs by 38%, and the labour content per vehicle by 63%, in order to effectively compete with Japanese imports in the domestic market during the 1980s. However, the capital required for such a massive retooling of the Canadian industry is

TABLE 5-3

Estimated Flow of Funds Between U.S. Parent and Canadian Affiliates in Total Manufacturing 1966-80

(in millions of current U.S. $'s)

	1966	1967	1968	1969	1970	1971	1972	1973	1974	1975	1976	1977	1978	1979	1980
Outflows from Canada															
Fees and royalties	161	177	186	186	196	211	256	298	396	400	452	546	595	658	713
Net interest paid	25	35	43	41	46	43	54	57	58	56	70	76	79	105	197
Gross dividends	294	221	202	155	265	300	330	433	494	523	625	676	661	852	665
Total outflows	480	433	431	382	507	554	640	788	948	979	1,147	1,298	1,335	1,615	1,575
Inflows into Canada															
Retained earnings	285	334	442	610	339	574	770	1,008	1,298	1,106	1,202	543	754	1,156	1,040
Equity and intercompany account transfers	439	11	-4	260	234	-39	227	148	410	130	67	-229	165	455	365
Total inflows	724	345	438	870	573	535	997	1,156	1,708	1,236	1,269	314	919	1,611	1,405
Net capital flows (cumulative)	1966-70 = 717 inflow					1971-75 = 1,723 inflow					1976-80 = 1,452 outflow				
Net capital flows excluding transportation equipment industry	1966-70 = 598 inflow					1971-75 = 1,712 inflow					1976-80 = 387 outflow				

Note: Data included from incorporated affiliates only.

Source: U.S. Department of Commerce, Bureau of Economic Analysis, unpublished data from *United States Direct Investment Abroad.*

Source: Perry op cit. p.132.

considered unlikely to be forthcoming. The Canadian industry, because of its corporate and market integration with the US, will largely follow the lead of the US automotive industry. US policy presently places a premium on the repatriation of assembly line jobs back to the US, combined with disinvestment in Canada and the acquisition of higher cost parts in low-wage countries. As a result, it is concluded that Japanese imports are likely to capture some 50% of the Canadian automotive market by the mid-1980s and that the Canadian economy will have shed up to 70,000 automobile related jobs. In fact, the report cited is so pessimistic with regard to the future prospects of the Canadian automotive sector that it takes the unprecedented step of recommending that governments in Canada should begin planning now for the massive dislocation that will be caused by the restructuring of the Canadian automotive industry. The analysis makes it clearly evident that the Canadian auto industry can never again be expected to provide the requisite dynamic base for the expansion of manufacturing activity in Canada.

Furthermore, while the aforementioned developments were taking place on the domestic scene the world economy was also changing. During the 1970s, some very important shifts in the location of production facilities and in the structure of world demand for manufactured products, were also occurring. The developing nations, struggling to achieve economic progress, have moved aggressively into the manufacture of labour intensive products. Countries such as South Korea, Singapore, Taiwan and Brazil have now established highly competitive manufacturing sectors in labour intensive products through the provision of generous concessions to large multinational enterprises. This policy proved highly successful, since it fitted in with the global strategy, pursued by most multinationals during the 1970s, to shift the manufacture of low skill, labour intensive products to countries with relatively low labour costs, in order to enhance their competitive position in the markets of the developed nations.

The most advanced industrialized nations have accordingly responded to this transfer of labour intensive manufacturing activity to low wage countries by gradually phasing out their own labour intensive industries and by channeling all of their available resources into the manufacture and export of technology intensive products, which are not as sensitive to labour cost differentials. Unfortunately, Canada has been unable to follow suit. Lacking the R&D base and domestic technological capability required to competitively manufacture and export high technology products, Canada has had little alternative other than to rely on exchange rate adjustments and tariffs to stem the decline of mature labour intensive industries and to protect the cost competitiveness of Canada's traditional primary manufacturing sector.

However, the efforts are clearly subject to diminishing returns. The structure of world demand for manufactured products has shifted significantly during the last decade, away from commodities in which Canada possesses a well developed manufacturing capability and towards those products in which Canada has relatively pronounced disadvantages. During the 1960s, international demand for manufactured products, such as electrical appliances, automobiles, non-ferrous metals, paper, iron and steel, as well as heavy electrical equipment, increased at a brisk pace, thus facilitating the expansion of these industries in Canada (Figure 5-4). However, since 1970, world demand for these products has grown much more slowly. In fact, the only products that have maintained consistently high growth rates throughout the 1970s are the very ones in which Canada has traditionally recorded large trade deficits, due to our lack of indigenous technological capability in the manufacture of R&D intensive goods. Furthermore, since these technology intensive industries will also likely be the growth industries of the 1980s, our lack of capability in this area will almost certainly place an additional constraint on the further expansion of manufacturing activity in Canada, regardless of the external value of the Canadian dollar or the tariff protection which is fast disappearing.

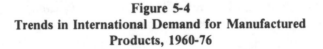

Figure 5-4
Trends in International Demand for Manufactured
Products, 1960-76

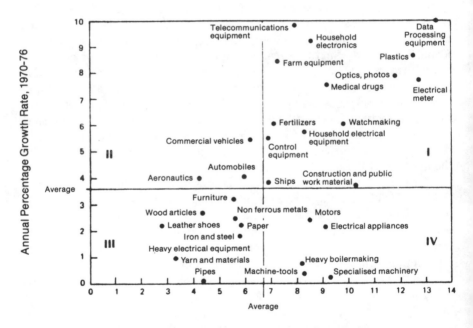

Annual Percentage Growth Rate, 1960-70

Source: OECD, DSTI/IWD/FIS/80.22/Annex.

(b) The Service Sector

The Canadian economy, like most other industrial economies, has undergone profound changes since the end of the Second World War. This is particularly evident in the changing distribution of employment that has occurred among the major sectors of the economy. During the last three decades, the focus of economic activity has shifted significantly away from the goods producing and toward the service sector of the economy. Thus, while employment in the non-agriculture sector of the economy increased by approximately six million jobs from 1950-1979, 80 percent of this increased employment occurred in the service sector.

As a result of this increase, employment in the service sector now accounts for 2/3 of total employment in the Canadian economy. However, while the rapid growth of employment in service industries has been widely noted, there is, as yet, no consensus regarding the implications for future economic prospects and employment. To a large extent, this is due to the almost complete lack of knowledge concerning the characteristics and economics of the service sector in Canada and of the service economy in general.

The mystery that presently surrounds the service economy is mainly due to the many different types of economic activity comprised by this sector. The service sector is really an extension of the many diverse activities that range from traditional personal services such as laundry and restaurant services, to more specialized knowledge based industries providing banking and computer services. In addition, the service sector also encompasses non-commercial service industries such as government, hospitals, schools, and universities. Inevitably, with such a disparate array of service industries the relative importance of specific activities will differ significantly, thereby affecting not only the growth and performance of the service sector itself, but also that of the whole economy.

While total employment in the Canadian economy has more than doubled over the last 30 years, nearly 90 percent of this increase took place in the service sector. During this period, employment in the service sector more than tripled, rising from 2.2 million persons in 1950 to nearly 7.0 million by the end of 1979 (see Table 5-4). Moreover, it appears that the employment in the service sector has continued to expand at an average rate of some 4.0 percent per annum, regardless of the annual rate of growth in employment that has occurred in other sectors of the Canadian economy (Table 5-5).

As a result of these dramatic developments, the character of total employment in Canada, accounted for by goods producing and service producing industries, has also changed substantially. Table 5-6 shows the changes in the distribution of employment that have occurred between the goods and services producing sectors since 1950. In both the agriculture and industry segments of the goods producing sector the share of employment has declined

TABLE 5-4
Levels of Employment by Sector
Selected Years 1950-1982
(000)

	1950	1960	1970	1980	1982
Goods	2771	2696	2942	3514	3260
Agriculture	1018	682	491	479	462
Industry	1753	2014	4836	3035	2798
Services	2205	3269	4836	7194	7385
Total Economy	4976	5965	7778	10208	10645

TABLE 5-5
Average Annual Rates of Growth In Employment By Sector
1950-1980

	Agriculture %	Industry %	Goods %	Services %
1950-60	−3.8	1.7	0.0	3.8
1960-70	−3.5	2.4	1.2	4.2
1970-80	−0.2	2.4	1.9	4.8

TABLE 5-6
Distribution of Employment By Sector Selected
Years 1950-1982
Percentages

	1950	1960	1970	1980	1982
Goods	55.7	45.2	37.8	32.8	30.6
Agriculture	20.5	11.4	6.3	4.5	4.3
Industry	35.2	33.8	31.5	28.3	26.3
Services	44.3	54.8	62.2	67.2	69.4
Total Economy	100.0	100.0	100.0	100.0	100.0

Note: Goods producing industries include agriculture plus industry;

Industry includes manufacturing, construction and primary industries other than agriculture;

Services include transportation, communication and other utilities; wholesale and retail trade; finance, insurance and real estate; community, business and personnel service industries; and public administration.

Source: Based on data available from Statistics Canada, *Historical Labour Force Statistics*, cat<71-201, various years.

consistently over the last 30 years. In contrast, the share of total employment accounted for by the service sector has increased significantly, rising by more than 20 percentage points during this same period. In 1950, less than one out of every two persons was engaged in this sector. Moreover, by the end of 1980, service industries accounted for two out of every three persons employed in Canada.

The distribution of employment within the service sector has also changed significantly during the last 30 years. Two industries (community, business and personnel services; and finance insurance and real estate) have increased their respective shares of employment within the service sector, while two others (transportation, communication and other utilities; and wholesale and retail trade) have accounted for a declining percentage (Table 5-7). By 1980, approximately 43 percent of employment in the service sector was accounted for by community, business and personal services, 25 percent by wholesale and retail trade, 13 percent by transportation, communication and other utilities, 10 percent by public administration and about 8 percent by finance, insurance and real estate (Table 5-8).

Furthermore, while employment in the service sector increased by almost 5.0 million from 1950 to 1980, two industries, community, business

TABLE 5-7
Service Sector's Share of Total Employment 1950-1982
(%)

	1950	1960	1970	1980	1982
TRSCU	9.4	9.6	8.7	8.5	8.3
TRADE	13.9	17.0	16.6	17.1	17.4
FIRE	2.8	3.8	4.7	5.7	5.6
CBPS	13.5	18.6	26.0	28.9	30.8
PADM	4.7	5.8	6.2	6.9	7.2
TOTAL SERVICES	44.3	54.8	62.2	67.2	69.4

TRSCU: Transportation, Storage, Communications and Utilities
TRADE: Wholesale and Retail Trade
FIRE: Finance, Insurance and Real Estate
CBPS: Community, Business and Personal Services
PADM: Public Administration

Source: Based on data available from Statistics Canada, *Historical Labour Force Statistics*, cat. 71-201, various years.

TABLE 5-8

Levels of Employment in the Service Sector, Selected Years 1950-1982

(000)

	1950		1960		1970		1980		1982	
TRSCU	469	(21)	573	(18)	676	(14)	906	(13)	885	(12)
TRADE	690	(31)	1018	(31)	1303	(27)	1837	(21)	1848	(25)
FIRE	142	(7)	226	(7)	364	(8)	611	(8)	601	(8)
CBPS	670	(30)	1107	(34)	2025	(41)	3096	(43)	3284	(44)
PADM	234	(11)	345	(10)	486	(10)	744	(10)	767	(10)
TOTAL SERVICES	2205	(100%)	3269	(100%)	4836	(100%)	7194	(100%)	7385	(100%)

and personal services together with wholesale and retail trade, accounted for almost 75 percent of this increase. These two sectors of the economy have been by far the most important in terms of job creation within the Canadian economy during this period. From 1950 to 1980, employment in community, business and personal services increased by almost 2.4 million, while employment in the trade sector increased by over 1.1 million to 1.8 million. During the 1970s alone, employment in the former group increased by over 100,000 persons annually, with employment in the wholesale and retail trade sector increasing by almost 56,000 persons per annum.

However, a slightly different picture emerges when changes in the distribution of real output within the Canadian economy are examined. In contrast to the service sector's ever increasing share of total employment, the distribution of real output between goods and service producing industries in Canada has remained remarkably stable, particularly during the 1950s and 1960s (Table 5-9). Throughout this period, the service sector accounted for approximately 62 percent of real output and the goods sector 38 percent. During the 1970s, the service sector's share of real output increased modestly to 65 percent, with goods decreasing to 35 percent.

TABLE 5-9
Distribution of Real Domestic Product by Sector 1950-1982
(%)

	1950	1960	1970	1980	1982
GOODS	38.4	37.8	37.3	34.2	31.7
Agriculture	5.9	4.6	3.2	2.5	2.8
Industry	32.5	33.2	34.1	31.7	28.9
SERVICES	61.6	62.2	62.7	65.8	68.3
TOTAL ECONOMY	100.0	100.0	100.0	100.0	100.0

Furthermore, it appears that the share of real output, accounted for by the two service industries that have experienced the most rapid employment growth, has also remained virtually constant over the last three decades (Table 5-10). Between 1950 and 1980, employment in community, business and personal service activities increased from 13.5 percent to 28.9 percent of total employment in the Canadian economy. Yet, this sector's share of real output expanded by less than 1 percent during this same period. A similar trend is evident in the trade sector. During the last 30 years, the share of total employment accounted for by wholesale and retail trade increased from 13.9 percent to 17.0 percent, while the industry's share of real output remained relatively constant. This suggests that the rate of growth of productivity within the service sector has been much less than the overall rate of growth experienced by the rest of the domestic economy and, as a result, an ever increasing proportion of our labour force has been required to produce a constant share of real output in Canada.

In fact, the relatively poor productivity performance of the service industries has been largely responsible for the expansion of employment in this sector. Between 1950 and 1980, output per person in Canada increased by about 2.2 percent annually. However, the annual growth of output per person was 4.3 percent in agriculture, 3.1 percent in industry and only 1.0 percent in the service sector during this period.[27] Thus, for any given increase in real output, the employment requirements of the service sector have been substantially greater than those of the goods producing industries.

Nevertheless, it is now apparent that the introduction of new technologies, particularly in the field of information processing, will radically improve the productivity performance of service industries. Indeed, there are fears that the diffusion of micro electronics and other information technologies will generate an unprecedented wave of unemployment within the service sector. While it is unclear at this point whether the widespread application of these technologies will result in the massive unemployment predicted by some observers, it is evident that new developments will sharply curtail the

TABLE 5-10
Service Sector's share of Real Domestic Product 1950-1982
(%)

	1950	1960	1970	1980	1982
TRSCU	9.4	10.2	11.8	13.9	14.2
TRADE	12.1	12.0	11.8	12.7	12.2
FIRE	12.4	12.4	11.7	13.0	13.9
CBPS	19.2	18.1	19.9	19.3	20.6
PADM	8.5	9.5	7.5	6.8	7.3
TOTAL SERVICES	61.6	62.2	62.7	65.8	68.3

TRSCU: Transportation, Storage, Communication and Utilities
TRADE: Wholesale and Retail Trade
FIRE: Finance, Insurance and Real Estate
CBPS: Community, Business and Personal Services
PADM: Public Administration

Source: Based on data available from Statistics Canada, *Real Domestic Product by Industry*, cat. 61-213, various years.

growth of employment in service industries. As a result it is unlikely that the service sector in Canada will be able to continue to absorb the large number of workers that it has in the past.

c) Tourism: A Special Case

Despite the lack of attention often afforded to tourism, travel represents a very significant industry in Canada. Tourism is Canada's largest single employer, providing jobs for an estimated 900,000 Canadians or 8.5 percent of the labour force. Moreover, as a service industry, tourism is highly labour intensive and is frequently the sole source of employment and income available to Canadians in many small communities and relatively disadvantaged regions. Tourism is also Canada's sixth largest source of foreign exchange, surpassed only by the export earnings of major industries such as motor vehicles, forestry products and the oil and gas sector.[28] In 1981, the foreign exchange earnings of the tourism sector exceeded $3.7 billion. When this is added to the estimated $8.0 billion that Canadians spend annually on domestic travel, it becomes readily apparent that tourism is a very major sector within the Canadian economy.[29]

Tourism in Canada is also a potentially high growth industry. Travel has become a way of life in many countries and it is accorded a high priority by an ever increasing number of the public. In fact, during the 1970s, travel was the world's fastest growing industry. However, despite the generally buoyant demand for travel services that existed throughout the last decade, Canada's balance of payments on travel transactions deteriorated substantially in this period (Table 5-11). It appears that the major difficulties exist within the North American market. Historically, the large number of US residents that visit Canada annually, combined with the ever increasing number of Canadians travelling within Canada, have been the bulwark of the Canadian tourism industry. However, in 1975, our traditional travel surplus with the US shifted to a deficit that has remained high ever since.

While cyclical factors have been partially responsible for the expansion of Canada's travel deficit over the last ten years, they do not totally explain the developments. Surveys conducted by the Canadian government Office of Tourism and the Tourism Industry Association indicate that international travel is highly sensitive to relative changes in international income and price levels.[30] Income and price factors have been especially significant since 1974 in bringing about a substantial increase in the number of Canadians travelling to the US and a reduction in the number of Americans visiting Canada. From 1970 to 1976, per capita income in Canada increased much more rapidly than personal income in the US, which provided Canadians with more discretionary income to devote to travel than their US counterparts. In addition, during this same period, the general price level within Canada was also rising more rapidly than prices in the US, which made a Canadian holiday relatively more expensive for residents of both Canada and the US, than touring in the United

States. As a result, fewer Americans came to Canada and more Canadians opted for a holiday in the US. However, the 20 percent depreciation of the Canadian dollar that has occurred since 1977 has been more than adequate to offset these differences. Yet, despite these changes, Canada's overall travel deficit has remained high.

TABLE 5-11
Canada's Balance of Payments on the Travel Account
($000,000)

	1972	1974	1976	1978	1980	1981	1982
All countries							
Receipts	1230	1694	1930	2378	3349	3760	3724
Payments	1464	1978	3121	4084	4577	4876	5008
Balance	-234	-284	-1191	-1706	-1228	-1116	-1284
United States							
Receipts	1023	1328	1346	1650	2121	2491	2402
Payments	919	1196	1956	2552	2920	3208	3234
Balance	104	132	-610	-903	-799	-717	-872
Other Countries							
Receipts	207	366	584	728	1228	1269	1322
Payments	545	782	1165	1531	1657	1668	1774
Balance	-328	-416	-518	-803	-429	-399	-452

Source: Statistics Canada, *Travel Between Canada and Other Countries*, Cat. 66-201, Ottawa, 1982.

Another factor that is often cited in relation to Canada's tourism deficit is the harsh Canadian winter and the tendency for more and more Canadians to opt for a winter holiday in the south. However, as Table 5-12 clearly indicates, climatic conditions are only partially responsible for Canada's travel deficit. While revenues from foreign tourists fell significantly during the first quarter of the year, the travel payments of Canadians travelling abroad during the winter months accounted for less than 30 percent of Canada's total travel payments in 1981. Thus, it appears that the majority of Canadians travelling abroad still choose a holiday abroad in the spring and summer months, despite the favourable weather conditions that exist in Canada during this period.

The main problem may in fact turn out to be the amenities offered to tourists in Canada. The facilities, attractions and services provided by the Canadian tourist industry may not be meeting the needs and demands of the two major customers, viz. Canadians themselves and US visitors. Research undertaken for the Tourism Sector Consultative Task Force suggests that

TABLE 5-12
Quarterly Estimates of Canada's Balance of Payments
on the Travel Account
($000,000)

	1978	1979	1980	1981	1982
Receipts					
IQ	218	243	338	385	389
IIQ	619	772	877	991	983
IIIQ	1166	1410	1626	1815	1778
IVQ	375	462	508	569	574
TOTAL	2378	2887	3349	3760	3724
Payments					
IQ	1141	1163	1293	1394	1479
IIQ	1037	972	1093	1213	1276
IIIQ	1193	1073	1312	1352	1337
IVQ	713	747	879	917	916
TOTAL	4084	3955	4577	4876	5008
BALANCE					
IQ	−923	−920	−955	−1009	−1090
IIQ	−418	−200	−216	−222	−293
IIIQ	−27	377	314	463	+441
IVQ	−338	−285	−371	−348	−342
TOTAL	−1706	−1068	−1228	−1116	−1284

Source: See Table 4-11.

Canada is perceived to be offering relatively dull and uninteresting experiences that are lacking in the diversity required for an exciting holiday.[31] Much of Canadian tourism is presently based on the country's natural attractions and scenic landscape. Indeed, many tourists place a high priority on visiting Canada's national parks, but are prevented from building their entire holiday around the parks system often due to the lack of suitable facilities and accommodation. If the parks are to be used by visitors other than hikers and campers, then more comfortable indeed luxurious accommodation and more diverse activities (e.g., son et lumière shows) should be provided that cater to the tastes of the more demanding and cosmopolitan traveler. With an aging society (see Chapter 7) this clientele may be expected to become increasingly important. Policies concerning Canadian Park development and tourist facilities should be viewed within an overall tourism policy with a view to making the amenities more attractive and accessible to both Canadian and foreign tourists.

d) The Resource Sector

Given the predominant role that resources have traditionally played in Canadian economic development and the increased stress that will inevitably be placed upon resource industries during the 1980s this section will discuss Canada's major resource industries individually in order to assess development prospects, opportunities and possible constraints. The specific sectors examined comprise: agriculture, forestry, fisheries, minerals and the energy industry.

Agriculture

The agricultural sector is an important component of the economy in virtually every region of Canada. In 1981, over 480,000 persons were engaged in agricultural activities across Canada. The gross value of agricultural output exceeded $18.0 billion in Canada during 1981, with $8.4 billion of this production destined for export markets. As a rule, export sales of agricultural products usually account for more than 10 percent of Canada's total exports.

Moreover, it appears that the agricultural sector will be called upon to play an even greater role in the Canadian economy during the next 20 years. In a recent Cabinet Discussion Paper entitled *Challenge for Growth: An Agri-Food Strategy for Canada*, the federal Minister of Agriculture outlined a new policy initiative, that is designed to double Canadian agricultural production over the next 20 years through export led growth.[32] However, any attempt to increase significantly the volume of agricultural production in Canada would almost certainly aggravate the already deteriorating agricultural resource base. Among other things higher real prices for agricultural commodities are required to facilitate a significant increase in Canadian agricultural output, such price development would encourage the reactivation of large tracts of land that have been abandoned over the past years. During the last 100 years, increases in the volume of Canadian agricultural output have largely been achieved despite the abandonment of marginal land with inherently low productivity on the basis of the intensive exploitation of higher quality farmland through the application of ever increasing quantities of chemical pesticides, herbicides and fertilizers in order to enhance yields. There are approximately 69 million hectares of land in Canada that are well suited for agricultural purposes and virtually all of this land is now under cultivation. While an additional 60 million hectares have some agricultural potential, less than 5 million hectares are reasonably well suited for agricultural production.[33] Much of this marginal land is located in northern regions and subject to unfavourable soil and climatic conditions. As a result, yields per hectare are low and presently uneconomic to exploit. Thus, in the absence of a substantial increase in the price of agricultural commodities, any increase in Canadian output would have to be achieved through an even more intensive utilization of existing farmland.

As noted earlier, the intensification of agricultural land use, practised under expanding mono-culture systems in both western and eastern Canada, has already resulted in a substantial degradation of agricultural soils. Placing additional demands on existing farmland will only accelerate this deterioration. Soil salinity, which presently affects 10 percent of agricultural soils in the Prairie Region, is probably the most pervasive problem facing the agricultural sector today. It is believed that the effects of 80 years depletion of native vegetation and cultivation are now showing up over a steadily widening area. Soil salinization is caused by the dispersion of saline water, followed by evaporation and precipitation in or on the soil. Water movement between soil and shallow ground water can be altered by cultivation and removal of perennial vegetation, which is capable of greater transpiration than many agricultural crops. The problem is accentuated under summer fallow conditions, when no crop is grown at all. High levels of salinity reduce the germination and growth of most crops by interfering with water and nutrient transport mechanisms across soil-root interface.[34] Ultimately, as the build up of saline substances in soils increases, nutrient intake is severely reduced and crop growth stunted. Cereal and oilseed crops appear to be particularly susceptible to the effects of saline soil.

Moreover, this problem is increasing due to the widespread continuation of summerfallowing in the monoculture wheat belts of western Canada. For any given year, up to 25 percent of cultivated acreage in western Canada lies in summerfallow as a weed control measure, or as a substitute for crop rotation. In addition, while continuous cropping with monoculture cereal can help to prevent the build up of saline substance in soils, this practice tends to accentuate the loss of organic matter and nutrients in Prairie soils, which are already badly depleted as a result of summerfallowing. In fact, it appears that the only way to arrest soil salinization, without causing other undesirable side effects, is to engage in regular crop rotation utilizing forage crops as a substitute for cereals. However, under present agricultural policies and market conditions, planting forage crops and recycling animal residues back into the soil to replenish organic matter and nutrients is both inconvenient and uneconomic for most Prairie farmers.

The loss of organic matter and nutrients in Prairie soils is also a significant concern in itself, since up to 50 percent of the organic matter in many Prairie soils has already been lost due to over-tillage, continuous cropping and summer fallowing.[35] While almost any decline of the organic matter in mineral soils is of concern, the loss of organic matter in this region is particularly alarming given the high native nutrient budgets and low precipitation common in this area. Organic matter is a major factor in soil structure and a loss of structure reduces fertility, in addition to rendering soils more susceptible to wind erosion. Moreover, as organic matter levels decline under summerfallow or continuous cropping, increased fertilizer use is required to maintain crop yields.[36] However, the application of ever increasing doses of chemical fertilizers to soil also tends to accelerate the breakdown of native organic matter and nutrients, in addition to facilitating over-tillage. While crop rotations, incorporating a forage legume, or the use of manure, can reduce or even prevent the net loss of organic matter from cultivated soils, these practices are usually regarded as uneconomic in the monoculture wheat belts of Western Canada.

Intensive land use techniques have also resulted in the serious degradation of agricultural soils in Eastern Canada. Soil erosion by water is now the most widespread manifestation of soil degradation in this region. Erosion by water, moves or removes the nutrients needed for crop growth and causes the redistribution of soil particles, often resulting in the removal of organic matter and fine grained minerals. This process tends to leave parts of fields with shallow top soils, which retard water holding capacity and root development and ultimately lead to uneven crop growth.

Soil erosion in Eastern Canada did not become a significant problem until the area used for corn and other row crops started to increase in the early 1960s. However, the long term shift to the production of monoculture corn and soy beans, at the expense of hay and small grains crops, has greatly increased the vulnerability of agricultural land throughout the Great Lakes-St. Lawrence region to soil degradation by water erosion. The area most susceptible to water erosion is Southern Ontario, where soil has been subjected to continuous corn production; land erodes at rates of up to 12 T/ha (tons per hectare) annually.[37] In contrast, when corn is rotated with hay, erosion rates fall by as much as 50 percent. Moreover, the production of continuous corn on a 7 percent slope has been found to result in erosion rates as high as 19 T/ha, while in rotation with hay and oats, annual losses from corn production on a similar landscape did not exceed 1 T/ha. It is thus evident that the productivity of much prime agricultural land in Southern Ontario will be seriously threatened if improved management techniques such as contour and minimum tillage, ploughing and the use of crop rotations are not implemented in the immediate foreseeable future. However, these practices are not presently perceived as being economic under the intensive monoculture system of land use that has become prevalent in Eastern Canada. Factors related to the degradation of agricultural land are identified in summary form in Table 5-13.

Forestry

The forestry sector is by far the most important industry in Canada. In aggregate, the forest industry directly employs over 300,000 Canadians and is claimed to account indirectly for an additional 700,000 jobs. Thus, it is asserted that possibly over 1.0 million jobs or 1 job out of 10 in Canada is forestry related.[38] In 1980, the value of shipments of forestry products exceeded $22.8 billion and represented almost 14 percent of all manufacturing shipments in Canada. Moreover, the industry's export sales reached $12.8

billion in 1980 and accounted for 17.2 percent of all commodities exported from Canada. The industry is also by far Canada's largest net earner of foreign exchange, with net earnings of almost $12.0 billion in 1980.

In addition, the forestry sector is also a significant factor in the economy of many regions in Canada. More than 300 single industry towns right across Canada are totally dependent on the forest industry for their livelihood, and continued existence. Regionally, the industry accounts for over 30 percent of industrial value added in Atlantic Canada, 15 percent in Quebec, 7 percent in Ontario, 11 percent in the Prairies, and for over 50 percent in British Columbia.[39]

Table 5-13
Factors Related to the Degradation
of Agricultural Land in Canada

Past 100 Years	*The Next 100 Years*
1. Improvements in crop varieties, fertilizers and management, giving continual crop yield increases.	1. Yield benefits from variety and fertility improvements reaching a peak.
2. Increased inputs of inexpensive energy used for tillage, pesticides, fertilizers.	2. Energy costs rising rapidly—some sources discontinued.
3. Heavy reliance on native soil fertility and structure to resist abuse from continued intensive cropping.	3. Soil organic matter levels declining to reach new equilibria with cropping practices—lower fertility and soil structure less able to resist tillage abuse.
4. Marginal land abandoned in favour of better soils and domestic zones.	4. Probable need to return marginal land to agriculture use because of demand for food.
5. Drainage and irrigation developments in areas with greatest benefit/cost ratios.	5. Drainage and irrigation becoming less cost effective as lower capability soils used.
6. Urban expansion effects absorbed by combination of 1 and 2 above.	6. Land lost to urbanization replaced by lower capability soils, rather than by increasing yields in better soils.
7. Extensive use of crop rotations under mixed agricultural land use systems.	7. Increased intensification of land use practice under expanding monoculture systems.

Source: D.R. Coote et al, *An Assessment of the Degradation of Agricultural Lands in Canada*, Agriculture Canada, Ottawa, 1981, p.4.

Furthermore, despite the dominant role that the forest sector plays in the domestic economy, Canada has allowed its forestry resource base to decline to the point where there is now some question whether our remaining timber resources will be adequate to sustain the industry at its present level of production, let alone provide a basis for the continued expansion of this industry. It has always been customary in Canada to harvest available timber and leave nature to replenish the supply. In effect, Canada has mined its virgin forests and given too little thought to the availability of future timber reserves. As a result shortages of merchantable timber have emerged for just about every region of Canada, forcing governments to reduce annual allowable cuts (AAC) for softwood species by as much as 20 percent in recent years. Softwood accounts for approximately 94 percent of Canada's annual roundwood forest and presently constitutes our most critical supply problem.

While Canada's forests have been supposedly managed on a sustained yield basis for decades, with AACs defining an upper limit of harvest that can be sustained indefinitely, it is now apparent that this has not been the case. Over-exploitation of our forests has occurred due to a number of factors including the higher than anticipated losses to insects and forest fires and a general neglect for forestry renewal. Responsibility for misunderstandings and misinterpretations rests with both industry and government who have failed to differentiate clearly, until very recently, between commercial timber (i.e., timber that is economic to harvest), and the total volume of timber that exists in Canada.

For 1979/80, the AAC for softwood species in Canada was set at 173.8 million cubic metres (See breakdown in Table 5-14). The actual harvest was only 147.5 million cubic metres, indicating that a modest reserve for expansion of 26.3 million cubic metres remained. However, a more systematic analysis of this data by region has since revealed that over half of this theoretical reserve is located in exceedingly remote areas that are characterized by rough terrain and lack any of the infrastructure required for harvesting.[40] In short, this timber is at least in the immediate future, uneconomic. In addition, much of the remaining theoretical reserve is made up of forests that are either inadequately stocked or comprising species that are commercially unattractive or of poor quality. Most of this timber would also be uneconomic to harvest under present market conditions. Thus, in reality, Canada's timber harvest in 1979/80 is considered to approximate closely what may be the upper limit of timber that can be cut, on a sustained yield basis, under current market conditions.

Furthermore, local supply difficulties have already been experienced insofar as the readily accessible, relatively "free supply" of wood is rapidly declining or appears imminent in just about every region of Canada. While it has been estimated that the forestry industry on the B.C. coast has sufficient installed capacity to utilize just 90 percent of the AAC, when allowances are made for logging residuals and other factors, the potential annual resource

TABLE 5-14
Allowable Annual Cut of Softwoods on Production Forest Lands
(Thousand m³)

Province	AAC 1979	Harvest 1979/80	Surplus (Deficit)
Newfoundland	2,940	2,594	346
P.E.I.	150*	150	—
Nova Scotia	3,273	3,804	(531)
New Brunswick	6,790	7,577	(787)
Quebec	36,000	28,352	7,648
Ontario	26,720	17,529	9,191
Manitoba	6,076	1,715	4,361
Saskatchewan	3,500	3,230	270
Alberta	14,639	7,170	7,469
B.C.	73,483	75,199	(1,716)
Yukon	125*	125	—
N.W.T.	54*	54	—

*No allowable cut is published for softwood. This figure is the same as the average harvest shown on column two.

Source: Canadian Forestry Service, Ottawa.

depletion actually exceeds the present allowable cut.[41] Furthermore, the major portion of the timber reserve on the northern B.C. coast is uneconomic to operate. Large diameter sawlogs and veneer logs are available only at a premium in some areas of the B.C. interior. The situation on the Prairies is somewhat better. Alberta has by far the most promising outlook in terms of reserve potential, with one new forest products complex currently under construction and plans under consideration to open up new forest areas for development. However Saskatchewan's softwood timber harvest is already close to the AAC, which was recently reduced in recognition of future supply constraints. Manitoba has large areas of uncommitted timber, but limited volumes per hectare and high delivery costs to existing mills limit their value.[42]

While Ontario appears to have a substantial uncommitted timber reserve available for expansion, most of this timber is located in remote northern areas and considered economically inaccessible at this time.

In addition, a reduction in Ontario's AAC has already been made and further reductions appear imminent due to the failure of a large portion of the province's cut over forests to properly regenerate. Shortages of large diameter softwood logs are already apparent in the areas from Thunder Bay in the northwest to Pembroke in the northeast.[43] Quebec's situation is similar to that of Ontario. The province's softwood AAC is about 25 percent above the present harvest. However, two-thirds of this hypothetical reserve is located in the uninhabited forests north of Port Cartier and the Ontario border. Extraction costs in this region would be high due to difficult terrain and the absence of adequate infrastructure.[44] Local shortages also exist in the province, particularly for prime sawlogs.

The softwood deficits in Atlantic Canada are already well known. In New Brunswick, the existing industry has annual capacity to utilize 25 percent more wood than can be harvested on a sustained yield basis, given existing levels of forest management. Repeated budworm infestations have severely damaged the growing stock in New Brunswick, and this situation is more serious in the Cape Breton region of Nova Scotia.[45] The present harvest in both of these provinces is currently running at about 15 percent above the estimated AAC. Newfoundland has also been hard hit by spruce budworm infestations, which could result in further reductions in the province's AAC. While there is a modest reserve for expansion in Labrador, this timber would be very expensive to deliver to areas of local deficit on the island.[46]

The provinces themselves are largely responsible for the situation that has evolved. Under the BNA Act the provinces were assigned responsibility for the management of Crown forests within provincial boundaries. In addition, the provinces, collectively, own directly almost 90 percent of Canada's commercial timber land.[47] Proceeds derived from the sale of commercial timber rights constituted an important source of revenue for provincial governments in the early days of Confederation and continue to make a significant contribution to the incomes of some provinces today. Regardless of whether individual provincial governments have maintained responsibility for the rejuvenation of cut over forests themselves, or have assigned it to licensees, the level of forestry management practised in most regions of Canada has been grossly inadequate until quite recently.

During the last 50 years, efforts at forest renewal undertaken by the provinces, have remained relatively meagre, partly because of the confidence that timber reserves were virtually limitless and partly because of the reluctance to lay out capital. Despite increasing recognition in recent years by all governments in Canada of the impending timber shortages that we will face in the not too distant future, present forestry renewal efforts are still insufficient to ensure that Canada will have adequate timber reserves in the future to foster the continued expansion of the forestry industry. For example, in 1979/80, the industry harvested about 800,000 hectares of timber. While 200,000 hectares of this cut-over area have since been replanted or seeded, the remainder has been left to regenerate on its own. Approximately 200,000-300,000 hectares of this residual timber land should rejuvenate reasonably well naturally. However, the remaining 200,000-300,000 hectares will likely generate non-commercial weed trees or scrub unless some action is taken.[48] Moreover, little has been done as yet to return past neglected cut over lands or decadent stands to productive status, in spite of the fact that many of these sites are located a relatively short distance away from existing processing plants.

Fortunately, this situation can still be rectified. There are three distinct options presently open to Canada that would augment future timber supplies in most regions. They include:

1) Closer utilization of available forests in areas that are now being harvested;

2) Extension of harvesting activities into more remote or less attractive areas;

3) More intensive forest management to increase growth rates in presently harvested forests.

It has been estimated that by moving to a closer utilization standard, the annual recovery of softwood in Canada could be increased by 10-20 percent over present harvest levels.[49] However, this assumes total utilization of stands that are presently by-passed due to potentially low yields per hectare, small tree size or unattractive species mix. In addition, present logging systems could not recover much of this residual harvest efficiently and existing manufacturing plants would require costly modifications to process this timber. As a result, attempting to alleviate Canada's present supply problems through the adoption of a closer utilization standard would require substantial investment by the industry in new plant and equipment that would adversely affect its present competitive position.

Turning to the periphery in order to augment future timber supplies would require the opening up of large tracts of remote forests that are presently regarded as uneconomic by the industry. Investment in access roads, new communities and associated infrastructure would be necessary to bring these areas into production. These investments would probably call for large public subsidies in the harvesting of this timber, but the justification of such use of public funds may not prove to be acceptable in times of continuing pressures for the containment of expenditures from public funds. The industry itself would experience sharply higher operating costs in Canada's northern forests due to the rugged terrain and less attractive softwood species common in these regions. Indeed, industry may view such increases in cost economically unattractive and therefore unacceptable. In any case, such solution would probably be the most costly alternative available to Canada.

A shift away from present forestry management practices and towards more intensive management techniques, would yield much more substantial gains than the other two options combined and probably at a lower overall cost. Experience in northern forests elsewhere suggests that gains of 50-100 percent in wood volumes can be achieved under a sustained program of intensive forestry management that emphasizes the artificial regeneration of cut over stands.[50] Moreover, the adoption of intensive forestry management techniques would yield benefits in both the short and longer term. In the short run, the adoption of intensive management practices could provide for an immediate increase in the amount of timber available to the industry through the raising of the levels of the "allowable cut," which is defined as an increase in the present permissible harvest of mature timber based on the assumption that higher yields will result in the future from managed stands. This increment to the existing supply could be achieved for the current extraction cost plus the cost of implementing a forestry management program. In the long run intensive forestry management would yield even greater benefits in terms of cost savings through higher yields per hectare harvested, lower transportation costs to existing mills and more uniform tree size. In addition, high value future crops could be assured through seeding with only economically attractive species.

The forestry sector plays a vital role in the Canadian economy, and will very likely be called upon for an even greater contribution in the future for purposes of redressing Canada's severe balance of payments problem. There appears to be scope and a need for some major federal initiatives, in order to ensure that a sustainable program of forestry renewal and intensive forestry management is implemented as soon as possible. Moreover, the federal government could use the leverage of the purse to bring about the requisite transition and to ensure active federal involvement in the management and protection of Canada's forests.

Fisheries

The commercial fisheries sector is also a significant industry in the Canadian economy. In 1981, the total value of fish landings in Canada reached almost $800 million. In addition, the fishery industry employs over 100,000 Canadians and is often the only source of employment and income available in many remote regions of Atlantic Canada. The value of Canadian exports of fish products exceeded $1.5 billion in 1981.[51]

However, despite the importance of the fishery industry as a source of income and employment, based on a renewable natural resource, both of Canada's two major commercial fisheries in the east as well as the west, are in a state of crisis. Many commercial fishermen and fish processing plants are near bankruptcy and the fisheries industry continue to place a heavy burden on the Canadian taxpayer. A recent study of Canada's Pacific fishery industry concluded that our salmon stocks, by far the industry's most valuable resource, are now seriously depleted due to an inadequate level of fisheries management in the past that has encouraged overfishing.[52] While annual landings of Pacific salmon continue to dominate the West Coast fishery in terms of both volume and value, the present harvest has fallen to just 50 percent of the estimated maximum annual sustainable yield.[53]

For the five species of salmon on the Pacific Coast, the basic objective of Canadian fisheries management policy has always been to control harvesting, in order to ensure that a sufficient number of spawners escape, to regenerate stocks. However, with respect to salmon, the information base employed by fisheries authorities on stock ages and population dynamics has, until very recently, been so inadequate that escapement targets represented little more than educated guesses. Working with insufficient knowledge concerning salmon stocks and their spawning requirements and under heavy pressure from competing groups of fishermen, management of Canada's salmon fishery has often degenerated to nothing more than a series of attempts to satisfy the demands of various user groups without visibly harming the resource.[54] As a result, limits on the annual salmon catch have been consistently inflated, which has led to the serious depletion of salmon stocks.

Moreover, past attempts to limit access to our dwindling salmon stocks have been largely unsuccessful. Prior to 1969, there was no limit placed on the number of salmon fishing privileges granted on the West Coast. However, in 1969 a freeze was placed on the number of boats licensed to harvest salmon in response to a perceived decline in stocks. Unfortunately, much of the industry circumvented these new regulations by trading in existing craft for larger and more sophisticated vessels to enhance fishing capacity. When further restrictions were placed on the absolute size of fishing vessels in the mid 1970s, many fishermen responded by acquiring faster, more efficient vessels that were capable of harvesting a substantially greater catch despite their smaller size. Thus, in spite of repeated attempts to limit the size of the Pacific salmon fleet, the catching power or capacity of the industry continued to increase unabated throughout the last decade, placing ever increasing pressure on salmon stocks.

Today, the West Coast salmon fleet has more than doubled the capacity required to efficiently harvest the annual salmon catch. As a result, the economic returns available to all participants in the industry are severely depressed and excessive pressure continues to be exerted on salmon stocks.

In contrast, fish stocks on the East Coast are more than adequate to sustain the industry at its present level of activity. In fact, by 1987 the annual ground fish harvest in Atlantic Canada could reach 1.1 million tonnes, representing an increase of 370,000 tonnes over present levels.[55] However, despite the existence of this ample resource base, the Atlantic fishery is, if anything, in worse condition than the salmon fishery on the West Coast. The Atlantic fishery is presently in the throes of a deep financial and economic crisis, from which it is unlikely to emerge without large and continued injections of public funds.

The present financial plight of the fish processing industry on the East Coast is illustrative of what has been occurring throughout the Atlantic fishery since 1978. During this period, the industry has sustained massive losses. The severity of this financial crisis became evident in 1981, with the temporary closure of a number of large fish plants. Late in 1981, the federal government provided $15.0 million in short run assistance to the processing sector, but by year's end a number of companies had approached both federal and provincial governments for further relief.[56] The financial position of many of these companies has deteriorated further in 1982. From 1978-1981, net income in the processing sector, in relation to sales revenue, fell by more than 10 percentage points and pre-tax income plummeted by 14.2 percent (Table 5-15). In addition, while the high interest rates of 1981 and 1982 contributed to the industry's financial difficulties, interest rates and the heavy debt load experienced by many processors since 1978, are not the principal cause of the industry's problems. The major reason for the declining viability of the fish processing sector in Atlantic Canada is the shrinking gross margin in sales experienced during this period. Put simply, the industry's production costs have risen faster than its sales revenue, resulting in a classic cost/price squeeze that threatens to decimate much of the East Coast fishery unless relief is forthcoming.

However, there is very little that can be done by the industry itself, or by government, to alleviate this situation over the short or medium term. In most industries the typical way to increase gross margins, and thus restore profitability, is either to reduce production costs, or to increase selling prices. Unfortunately, neither of these options is presently open to the Atlantic

TABLE 5-15
Consolidated Income Statement for Sample of Fish Processors
in Atlantic Canada*
(All Figures Expressed as a Percent of Sales)

	1978 (%)	1981 (%)	Difference (in percentage points)
Sales	100.00	100.0	
Cost of Goods Sold	80.9	88.0	7.1
Gross Margin	19.1	12.0	−7.1
Other Income	.8	1.1	.3
Selling & Admin. Exp.	8.5	9.9	1.4
Long-term Inter.	1.3	2.8	1.5
Short-term Inter.	.9	4.8	3.9
Depreciation	2.2	2.8	.6
Pre-Tax Income (Loss)	7.0	(7.2)	−14.2
Tax	2.4	(.8)	− 3.2
Extraordinary Items	—	.4	.4
Net Income (Loss)	4.6	(6.0)	−10.6

* Sample comprised 80 percent of fish processing capacity in Atlantic Canada.

Source: Task Force on Atlantic Fishery, *Navigating Troubled Waters: A New Policy for the Atlantic.*

fishery. Material (fish) and direct labour costs account for approximately 90 percent of the manufacturing costs associated with fish processing in Atlantic Canada.[57] Since the earnings of most fishermen in this region are already close to the poverty line, any attempt to reduce material costs would be strenuously resisted by the harvesting sector itself and by the two levels of government that have been subsidizing the East Coast fishery for decades.[58] Moreover, wage rates in the processing sector are anything but excessive. Nor does the industry have much room to manoeuvre in order to achieve cost reductions through increases in operating efficiency. The excess capacity that characterizes this industry throughout much of the year is necessary to cope with the seasonal landings by the onshore fishery that peak during the summer months. Any move by the fish processors to achieve economies through closing down the marginal plants that cater to the onshore fishery would also be resisted by governments concerned with processing jobs and maintaining the viability of fishing villages.

The Atlantic fishery is also not in a position to unilaterally raise prices in the market segments in which it competes. Flat selling prices for fish products, during the last five years, have been primarily responsible for the difficulties that the industry has experienced and real prices for the products that the Atlantic fishery markets are not expected to increase over the medium term.[59] More than 50 percent of the industry's output is sold in the United States. However, unlike the industry's principal rivals in Iceland and Scandinavia, the East Coast fishery has specialized in the production of medium quality, price sensitive fish products, the so-called value for money market segment, where the negotiation is toward low cost and acceptable quality (Figure 5-5).[60] The industry's major competition in this market segment comes from the lower quality fish products sold in the US and Canada by Latin American, South Korean and Alaskan producers and from alternate sources of low cost protein such as chicken, pork and lower quality cuts of beef. Thus, if the Atlantic fishery attempts to raise its prices in this market, it would lose sales and market share to all of these competitors.

In contrast, producers in Iceland and Scandinavia have specialized in serving the high quality, non-price sensitive segment of the North American fish market where price premiums for quality of up to 30 percent are not uncommon.[61] Although Canadian producers would also like to serve this higher price, quality sensitive market and in fact must move aggressively into this market segment if the industry is ever to become economically viable, they presently lack the products required to do so, due to the lower average quality of ground fish landed at the dock in Atlantic Canada, and the inadequate attention paid to quality in processing plants.[62] Presently, less than 20 percent of the industry's harvest is suitable for quality conscious markets in either Canada or the US. As a result, producers from Scandinavia and Iceland are expected to continue to dominate this market segment over the medium term, leaving the Atlantic fishery little alternative but to continue producing high

Figure 5-5
Market Niches in the U.S. Frozen Ground Fish Market

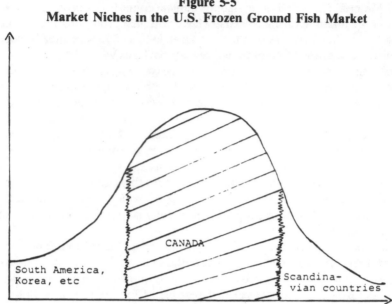

Quality and Price

Source: Task Force on Atlantic Fisheries, *Navigating Troubled Waters: A New Policy for the Atlantic Fisheries*, Supply & Services Canada, Ottawa, December 1982, p.51.

volume, lower quality fish products that cannot be economically processed under the industry's present cost structure.

Moreover, the Kirby Commission study of the Atlantic fishery has recommended that the industry engage in generic promotion and institute measures to improve the quality of its output, in order to enhance the price and quality of Atlantic fish products. These initiatives, even if successfully implemented, will only yield benefits over the long run. In the short and medium term, the Atlantic fishery will continue to serve as little more than an instrument for subsidizing job creation, requiring on-going injections of public funds.

Minerals

The non-fuel minerals sector has long been a mainstay of the Canadian economy. Although the industry experienced relatively slow growth during the last decade, the value of Canadian mineral production in 1980 amounted to $13.9 billion. When refined metal and other fabricated mineral products are included, the industry's total output exceeded $31.4 billion.[63] In 1980, the minerals sector employed 274,000 persons in 260 mines, 230 mills, 16 smelters and 15 refineries located right across Canada. The value of Canadian exports of metal ores, concentrates and scrap, non-metallic minerals, nonferrous metals and iron and steel exceeded $12.3 billion in 1980 and accounted for 16.5 percent of Canada's total export earnings.[64]

Unlike the situation that exists in several of Canada's other major resource industries, our minerals resource base appears to be more than adequate to sustain this industry well into the next century. As Figure 5-6 indicates, Canada's existing commercial reserves for most minerals are more abundant now than in 1974, despite the level of exploitation that has occurred throughout this period. To a large extent, this phenomenon reflects the cyclical fortunes of commercial activities in the industry. During periods of rising prices and growing market opportunities, exploration activities accelerate and additions to commercial reserves are enhanced. In contrast, during a downswing, the industry usually curtails its exploration efforts and reserves are drawn down. Evidently, many ore bodies presently being mined in Canada have not yet been fully explored. Nor are unexplored "hypothetical" additional reserves included in the definition of current commercial reserves. Once sufficient economic volumes of ore are identified in a deposit, it is unnecessary to search for further reserves until they are required. In most major mines, reserves are continually identified and at a rate capable of supporting further production for some 15-20 years ahead.[65]

Figure 5-6
Levels of Reserves

Metal contained in mineable ore, as of January 1 of each year

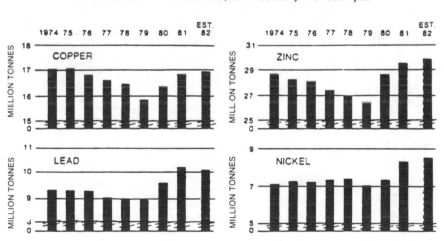

Note: Scale broken to allow annual differences to be emphasized

Source: Mineral Policy Sector, EMR, Canadian Mines Perspective from 1981, MR 192

Figure 5-7
Sources of Future Mine Supply

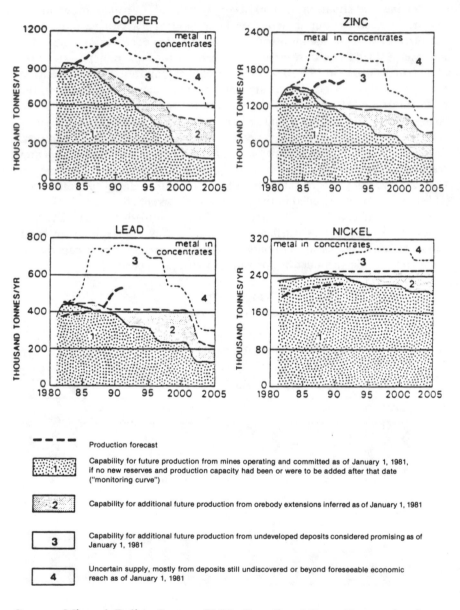

Source: Mineral Policy Sector, EMR Canadian Mines: Perspective from
1981, MR 192.

In fact, copper is the only major mineral produced in Canada in which future supplies appear uncertain beyond 1990 (Figure 5-7). However, this should not be taken as an indication that Canada will run out of copper reserves in the 1990s. As already noted, the process of proving up and exploiting mineral reserves is a dynamic rather than static phenomenon that responds fairly promptly to shifts in market conditions. For example, higher real prices for copper ores and concentrates over the next decade could trigger an increase in exploration activity in more remote regions of Canada that have previously been ignored due to the potentially high exploration costs and the development of known existing copper reserves that are presently regarded as sub-economic or marginal at current prices. In addition, any improvement in mining technology that lowered the economic cut-off point for the grade or depth of copper deposit that can be economically exploited at current prices would also render many Canadian copper deposits, that are presently considered sub-economic, viable to develop in the future.

Moreover, despite the lower average grade of ore mined in Canada, the Canadian minerals sector is presently in a very favourable competitive position vis-à-vis its major rivals in both the developed and developing nations.[66] As a rule, the most important determinant of cost competitiveness in the mining sector is the type and grade of ore exploited. Higher grade ores require less effort to extract and significantly less processing. However, the lower average quality of Canadian ores has not seriously affected the industry's overall cost competitiveness, since this disadvantage is usually more than offset by the valuable co-products and by-products such as gold, silver, platinum, sodium, iridium, cobalt and selenium in major Canadian copper, nickel and zinc deposits. This, to a large extent, is responsible for Canada's relatively favourable overall competitive position among the world's major mineral producers (see Tables 5-16, 5-17). In fact, our cost competitiveness actually improved significantly in 1979 and 1980 due to the large increase in precious metal prices and in the price of cobalt and molybdenum.[67] As a result, Canada is still the world's lowest cost producer of nickel.

In addition, while Canadian labour costs in the mining sector are among the highest in the world (Table 5-16), this disadvantage is totally offset by the lower energy costs enjoyed by Canadian producers. Since the dramatic increase in world oil prices, energy costs have become a major competitive factor in the minerals sector, due to the high energy intensity of extracting and processing ores. Energy, as a component cost, has made, and will continue to make, a positive contribution to the competitive position of the Canadian minerals industry during the 1980s. The government is generally intent upon keeping domestic oil prices competitive with world prices.[68] Canada is well endowed with other sources of reasonably priced energy as well such as natural gas, hydroelectric power and coal and has an excellent nuclear energy potential. In consequence it is considered desirable that the competitive

TABLE 5-16
Index of Unit Cost of Nickel Production in Selected Countries
(Total Cash Cost for Canada in 1980 = 100)

	Canada	Australia	Dom. Rep.	New Cal.	Philippines	Indonesia
CASH OPERATING COST						
Energy	10	42	74	66	86	33
Labour	66	37	18	52	4	6
Material & Supplies	23	26	26	26	28	22
Overhead, etc.	13	10	13	14	3	8
Total	112	115	131	158	121	69
Further Processing	—	7	—	10	—	20
Less Byproduct Production Cost	(27)	(5)	—	(3)	(5)	—
Total Cash Operating Cost	85	117	131	165	116	89
Interest Expense	15	25	11	20	50	44
Total Cash Cost	100	142	142	185	166	133
Rank	1	3	3	6	5	2

Source: Energy, Mines and Resources Canada: Mineral Policy: A Discussion Paper, Supply and Services Canada, Ottawa, Dec. 1981, p.43.

advantage provided the Canadian mineral industry, through lower energy prices, should be maintained at least over the next decade.

However, despite the present favourable competitive position of existing domestic mines, the competitiveness of totally new mining complexes built in Canada is uncertain. Most of Canada's remaining commercial mineral reserves are located in more remote areas, far from existing infrastructure and are subject to unfavourable terrain and often severe climatic conditions. New mining areas awaiting development include the MacMillan Pass area of the Yukon and the north-eastern region of British Columbia. Development of these remote areas hinges on the provision of infrastructure. Suitable road access is required, as well as rail transportation lines, the construction of port facilities and new townsites. In fact, the infrastructure costs associated with developing these regions are expected to exceed the cost of the mining complexes that the infrastructure is intended to serve.[69]

In contrast, some relatively unexplored or more richly endowed Third World countries have unexploited deposits that are located reasonably close to already existing infrastructure (Chile, Peru and the Philippines). It is thus likely that Canada will experience a relative disadvantage in coming years in new mine development, as the site of future developments moves to more remote locations. Large public subsidies may be required to offset the high infrastructure costs associated with developing these reserves, in order to make such projects economically attractive to the private sector.

TABLE 5-17
Index of Unit Cost of Copper Production in Selected Countries
(Canada 1979 = 100)

	1973	1976	1979	Rank (1979)
Australia	138	69	69	2
Canada	86	45	100	4
Chile	179	138	131	6
Peru	145	145	134	7
Philippines	138	158	152	8
Papua New Guinea	72	117	59	1
South Africa	90	86	114	5
United States	134	176	193	10
Zaire	97	117	86	3
Zambia	141	183	179	9

Source: Energy, Mines and Resources Canada, *Mineral Policy: A Discussion Paper*, Supply and Services Canada, Ottawa, Dec. 1981, p.44.

Moreover, the further expansion of the Canadian minerals sector will also be severely constrained by future international market conditions. Economic growth in the industrialized nations will be significantly lower in the 1980s than during the past two decades.[70] As a result, industrial production may be expected to expand only slowly, leading to a lower overall rate of growth in mineral consumption. In fact, it has been estimated that world demand for the major minerals that Canada produces will rise by just about 2-3 percent per annum during this period.[71] In addition, slow rates of growth in mineral consumption, combined with expected additions to global production capacity, may be expected to result also in continued depressed prices for minerals in the 1980s. World prices for nickel, lead and copper are forecast to increase only modestly, if at all, in real terms over the next 10 years.[72] A sustained regime of low mineral prices will, in turn, dampen exploration and development activities in the Canadian mining industry.

Canada's mineral industry will also face intensifying competition in the coming years as more countries develop their mineral resources or expand production capacity for export markets. However, perhaps the most significant structural change that is occurring within the international minerals industry, is the shift in ownership from international mining companies to host governments in the developing nations. This trend is particularly evident in copper production, where government enterprises now exercise control in Zaire, Zambia, Papua New Guinea, Chile and Peru, and have majority ownership in the Philippines and Mexico.[73] State ownership in the developing nations raises special concerns for mineral producers such as Canada and Australia that are largely dependent on market forces to guide mineral development. Due to their often desperate need for foreign exchange earnings from mineral exports, government controlled producers in the countries concerned are often pressured to sustain output when demand shrinks, placing additional downward pressure on world prices. Actions of this nature usually necessitate excessive production cut-backs in countries like Canada and thus further discourage new investment in the domestic industry. In addition, governments in developing nations have displayed a marked tendency in recent years to invest in new capacity based solely on social considerations, even when rates of return are low, such that new excess capacity is brought on stream, which destabilizes international mineral markets.

Canada's mineral exports may also be expected to face tariff barriers during the next decade in the markets of the developed nations and also increasingly in middle income countries with high market potential, that effectively preclude exports of processed mineral products from Canada.

Nominal tariff barriers are usually zero for mineral ores, but rise to higher levels as the degree of processing increases. These escalating tariff structures have become particularly prevalent in middle income or newly industrializing countries such as Brazil, Venezuela, Taiwan and South Korea, which have modelled their tariff schedules for mineral products on Japanese mineral tariffs. The true protective aspect of escalating tariffs is much higher than suggested by nominal rates, especially when the value added by a protected processing activity is relatively low. In addition, while the level of both nominal and effective protection in Japan, the US, and the EEC was reduced somewhat by the Tokyo Round of GATT negotiations, tariffs in the developed nations remained formidable barriers to Canadian exports of processed and fabricated mineral products.

Moreover, any attempt to enhance the value of Canada's mineral production through the further smelting and refining of ores and concentrates into processed mineral products prior to export, would have further deleterious effects on the environment. The sulphur dioxide emissions from existing non-ferrous metal smelters in Eastern Canada are the principal source of acid rain in this region, which is presently Canada's most pressing environmental problem. The costs associated with eliminating this environmental hazard already appear substantial. It has been estimated that achieving an 80 percent reduction of sulphur dioxide emissions from existing smelters, would cost upwards of $1.0 billion and would result in increased operating capital costs in excess of $200 million annually.[74]

While the "polluter pays principle" is now firmly entrenched in Canadian environmental policy-making, it would seem to be apparent, from the foregoing analysis of international market conditions, that the Canadian minerals industry will not be in a position to pass the cost of pollution abatement to their customers during the next decade. Nor does the industry appear to be capable of shouldering the entire cost itself, given the weakened financial conditions of many of Canada's major minerals producers (i.e. Inco, Noranda, Falconbridge). As a result, the provision of public funds will likely be required to assist in reducing the sulphur dioxide emissions from existing non-ferrous metal smelters in the medium term. Large public subsidies may also be required to facilitate the establishment of additional environmentally safe smelting capacity in Canada, if the government wishes to foster industrial development through further processing of Canadian minerals prior to export during the 1980s.

Energy

The energy sector is one of Canada's most richly endowed national resource industries and a source of strength in the economy. Canada's energy sector has experienced rapid growth during most of the post-war period and in the process has transformed Canada from a net importer, to a net exporter of primary energy. From 1945-73, the volume of Canadian energy production expanded rapidly, based largely on export led growth. For example, in 1973, Canada exported 60 percent of its petroleum production, 40 percent of its natural gas output and 6.4 percent of its electrical output to the United States.[75] However, with the decline in the production of conventional crude oil in Western Canada, during the mid-1970s, Canada's overall energy production fell until 1977.

Canada has been a net exporter of energy since 1969. Our overall trade surplus in primary energy has expanded almost continually throughout the 1970s, despite massive increases in the value of Canadian imports of crude petroleum after 1974. As Figure 5-8 clearly indicates, Canada's exports of natural gas and electricity have consistently exceeded our imports of crude petroleum, so that Canada's overall trade surplus in primary energy peaked at nearly $4.0 billion in 1979. While this surplus has since declined, as a result of continued increases in the price of crude oil imports, we still managed to register an overall surplus in primary energy trade of just over $3.0 billion in 1981.[76]

Figure 5-8
Canada's Dollar Trade in Energy Commodities, 1970-1979

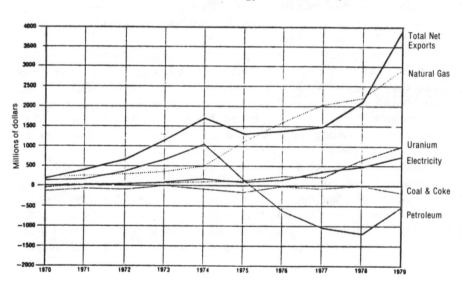

Source: After Canada, Department of Energy, Mines and Resources, 1980e. p.8.

It is crude petroleum that constitutes the only foreseeable energy problem in Canada. The basic difficulty, with respect to this commodity, is that production from conventional crude oil reserves in Western Canada will decline faster than overall demand throughout the 1980s, so that Canada will continue to depend on expensive imports of crude petroleum unless new sources of domestic supply are brought into production quickly. Production from conventional reserves in Western Canada is forecast to fall from 202,000 cubic metres per day in 1981 to 84,000 cubic metres per day by 1990, while domestic demand will decline from 284,000 cubic metres per day to 233,000 cubic metres per day.[77] (Under the metric system, 6:29 barrels of oil are taken as being equivalent to 1 cubic metre of oil.) In addition, while new-discoveries of conventional crude in Western Canada are almost certain to occur during this period, the western basin is recognized as a mature oil producing region that is unlikely to yield major new discoveries of sufficient magnitude to offset the decline in production from existing wells.

However, despite the somewhat discouraging forecast and the recent deferral of two major oil sands projects in Western Canada, our present difficulties in balancing crude oil supply and demand are considered to be largely transitory and should begin to disappear by the end of the decade (see Figure 5-9). For one thing, domestic demand has been declining more rapidly in recent years than was originally anticipated. Overall demand for crude petroleum in Canada fell by 2.3 percent in 1980 and 6.7 percent in 1981 in response to higher oil prices and accelerated rates of conservation and substitution.[78] Provided that this trend continues, our overall requirements for crude oil in the 1980s will fall below current projections. Moreover, the accelerated exploration activities in frontier regions, triggered by the National Energy Program (1980), has already yielded encouraging evidence that substantial reserves of crude petroleum exist on Canada Lands in the North and off the East-Coast. In particular, delineation of the Hibernia discovery off the coast of Newfoundland has proven up reserves of more than 1 billion barrels of oil, with excellent prospects for additional commercial reserves.[79] If a reservoir of 250 million cubic metres (1.5 billion barrels) is proven up as expected, this field could support the production of 40,000 cubic metres (250,000 barrels) per day for 15-20 years. In addition, further drilling in the Beaufort Sea-Mackenzie Delta region has produced evidence that the total oil and gas potential of this region would be equal to that of Hibernia. As Table 5-18 indicates, these two discoveries alone could prove adequate to make Canada self-sufficient in crude petroleum by 1990 if they are to be brought into production soon. However, this is doubtful, given the political difficulties between Ottawa and St. John's and the lack of commercial discoveries in the Beaufort Sea to date. Analysts now believe that oil self-sufficiency will not be achieved before the mid-1990s.

Furthermore, despite these initial discoveries, the untapped oil and gas potential of the Canadian frontier is expected to remain immense. The Geological Survey of Canada now estimates that the total oil and gas potential of Canada Lands is 4.6 billion cubic metres (29 billion barrels) of oil and 8.5 trillion cubic metres (300 trillion cubic feet) of gas. Specifically, there is major potential for additional oil discoveries on the East Newfoundland Shelf (1.3 billion cubic metres or 8.4 billion barrels); in the Beaufort Sea-Mackenzie Delta area (1.5 billion cubic metres or 9.4 billion barrels); and in the Arctic Islands region (700 million cubic metres or 4.3 billion barrels).[80] Even if only a fraction of these potential reserves are discovered and proven commercial,

Figure 5-9
Crude Oil Supply and Demand

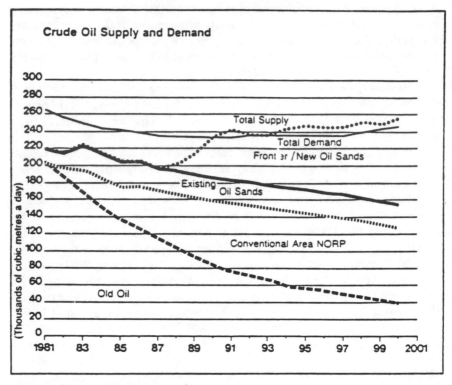

Source: Energy Update, op. cit.

production from Canada Lands would be more than adequate to make Canada self-sufficient in crude oil well into the next century.

In contrast to our diminishing reserves of crude oil, Canada's proven reserves of natural gas are extensive and have expanded almost continuously during the last two decades.[81] Despite the accelerated substitution of natural gas for oil heating, that has occurred in recent years, our annual net additions to gas reserves still exceed production and proven reserves continue to grow. This has resulted in a growing surplus of natural gas in Canada that is available for export, should market conditions and balance of payments considerations warrant such action. In fact, the extent of Canada's gas reserves in conventional areas alone is huge.

In a recent analysis of Canada's existing natural gas surplus, the National Energy Board concluded that Canada has existing proven reserves of natural gas in conventional areas in excess of 80 exajoules (76 trillion cubic feet) and forecast that net additions to reserves in Western Canada alone should exceed

44 exajoules over the next 20 years.[82] Canada's overall reserve potential in this region is now estimated at 183 exajoules or 171 trillion cubic feet. This compares with present Canadian consumption of natural gas of just 1.7 exajoules annually (1.6 trillion cubic feet), which is forecast to increase to only 3.3 exajoules per annum by the year 2000.[83] Moreover, these estimates of Canada's existing gas reserves do not make any allowance for the substantial quantities of natural gas believed to exist in frontier regions.

As a result of this review, the National Energy Board authorized the export of an additional 12.2 exajoules (11.5 trillion cubic feet) of natural gas from Western Canada between 1985-2001, in order to relieve the cash flow difficulties of gas producers, caused by carrying such a large inventory of unsold gas. Over the life of these export licenses, authorized shipments of natural gas are expected to generate net export earnings of approximately

TABLE 5-18
Canada
Estimated Crude Oil Supply and Demand
(Thousand Cubic Metres per day)

	1981			1990*
DEMAND	265	DEMAND		233
TOTAL PRODUCTION	220	PRODUCTION WESTERN CANADA		
		Existing Wells	84	
CHANGE IN STOCK	−4	Enhanced Recovery	20	
		New Discoveries	47	
NET IMPORTS	41	Experimental	3	
		Sub-Total	154	
		PRODUCTION CANADA LANDS		
		Hibernia	(40)	
		Beaufort Sea	(40)	
		Sub-Total	(80)	
		TOTAL PRODUCTION		234
		NET IMPORTS		−1

( ) Estimate

* It is now accepted that oil self-sufficiency will not be achieved by 1990 since significant production from the Canada Lands will occur only well into the 1990s.

Source: Based on data available from Energy, Mines and Resources Canada.

$70.0 billion.[84] However, despite the authorization of these additional export sales, it is clearly evident that Canada will still have substantial volumes of surplus natural gas available for export during the next decade as potential reserves are proven up and added to the existing reserve inventory. Thus, should Canada continue to experience balance of payments difficulties in the 1980s, surplus natural gas will be available for export in order to alleviate any undue pressure placed on the domestic economy through either the capital or current account.

Canada is also blessed with abundant hydro-electricity reserves in comparison with just about any other nation. Electricity presently plays a key role in Canada's energy grid as a potential substitute for oil and as an important source of export earnings to offset the cost of crude oil imports. In 1981, Canada's net export earnings derived from the sale of electricity to the United States reached $1.1 billion.[85] Moreover, as Table 5-19 clearly indicates, Canada has sufficient undeveloped hydro-electric power potential that is both economically and technically viable to more than double our current output of electricity generated through hydro-electric installations.

In addition, aside from our physical capacity to generate electricity, Canada has also developed one of the world's best nuclear electrical generating systems—the CANDU nuclear reactor. The control and perfection of this technology provides Canada with an alternative source of reasonably priced electricity that can be utilized in future years to make up for any domestic shortfall in hydro-electric power and gives Canada the option of exporting large quantities of electric power.

However, energy developments are associated with a variety of environmental impacts ranging from changes in wildlife habitats to possible climatic changes resulting from large scale developments such as James Bay hydro-electric development, impacts which will have to be considered before decisions to proceed with projects are made.

Infrastructure

By far the most pressing infrastructure issue presently confronting the resource sector is the provision of adequate transportation facilities for resource related products. In particular, the provision of adequate rail transportation services has become a matter of special concern to the minerals sector, the forestry industry and the agricultural sector. These three industries are the principal users of Canada's railways and are often forced to compete with each other for available rail capacity. The minerals industry alone accounts for 60 percent of all railway freight in Canada, with forestry and agricultural products accounting for the bulk of other rail shipments.[86] In recent years troublesome bottlenecks in the rail system have become increasingly frequent, especially in the areas west of Thunder Bay, where large volumes of coal, potash, forest products and grain have combined to place considerable stress on Canada's existing rail capacity. In fact, concern has

TABLE 5-19

Canada's Hydro-Electric Power Potential in 1980

(Electrical Megawatts)

	Actual Operation or Under Construction	Remaining Theoretical Potential	Remaining Technically Developable Potential	Remaining Technically & Economically Developable Potential
Nfld. & Labrador	6,535	7,000	6,272	4,776
PEI	—	—	—	—
Nova Scotia	360	160	100	50
New Brunswick	900	620	556	460
Quebec	25,750	42,160	30,750	18,838
Ontario	7,138	7,770	6,152	2,072
Manitoba	4,796	7,023	4,945	4,945
Saskatchewan	567	2,395	1,711	1,161
Alberta	718	18,800	11,440	4,357
British Columbia	12,134	29,400	25,827	17,575
Yukon	68	11,000	10,440	5,043
N.W.T.	47	14,900	6,000	4,163
CANADA	59,103	141,228	104,193	63,440

Source: Report of the Special Committee on Alternative Energy and Oil Substitution to the Parliament of Canada, *Energy Alternatives*, Supply and Services Canada, Ottawa, 1981. p.35.

already been expressed that access to the existing system may have to be rationed in the mid-1980s unless rail facilities in Western Canada are expanded and upgraded.[87]

Until very recently, the major impediment to expanding and upgrading the rail system in Western Canada has been the Statutory Crow's Nest Pass Freight Rate applied to grain shipments from the Prairies. The "Crow Rate," which was first established in 1897, provides for reduced freight rates on grain and flour shipments coming out of Western Canada by rail. While this special rate was originally established to foster the expansion of the western grains economy, it has also served to preclude any significant expansion or upgrading of the western rail transportation system. During the last decade, payments by grain producers under the "Crow Rate" have averaged less than 20 percent of the actual cost of hauling grain to major markets.[88] The mounting losses sustained by Canada's two railways on grain traffic has severely reduced their cash flow in recent years and diminished their ability to even maintain existing lines, let alone invest in additional capacity to accommodate ever-increasing volumes of rail traffic in Western Canada. For example, in 1981/82, CN and CP experienced a combined revenue shortfall in excess of $650 million as a result of being required to haul grain at the artificially low "Crow Rate."

In addition to constraining the expansion of the rail transportation network, the "Crow Rate" has also retarded the further development and diversification of the western agricultural economy. Major grain export sales were lost in 1977/78 and again in 1978/79 as a result of insufficient transportation capacity to move grain to points of exit.[89] Although low volumes of other bulk commodities permitted a record grain movement in 1981/82, the demand for transportation capacity from coal, potash, sulphur, forest products and other commodities will increase when the economy recovers, effectively preventing any further expansion of grain sales unless additional rail capacity is forthcoming.

The "Crow Rate" has also favoured the production of raw grain in the Prairie region at the expense of local feed grain usage, livestock production, alternate crop development and agricultural processing. Feed grain prices in Western Canada are up to $20 per ton higher than would otherwise be the case, because of distortion in freight rates charged.[90] Thus, western grain using industries such as livestock production, feed milling and meat packing are forced to pay relatively higher prices for their principal inputs which reduces their profitability and incentive to expand. Diversification into the production of non-Crow crops has also been discouraged, due to the relatively higher transportation charges, and lower farmgate prices, that alternate crops face. Moreover, continuous cropping with monoculture grain has been encouraged under the "Crow Rate," despite the extensive damage to Prairie soils caused by this practice. Artificially low transportation charges for moving grain have also had an adverse effect on other natural resource industries in Western

Canada, since these industries have been forced to pay higher freight rates and to accept a lower level of rail service, in order to partially offset losses incurred by the railways in transporting grain.

In response to the deteriorating condition of the rail transportation network in Western Canada, the Federal Government has changed the Statutory Crow Rate in order to facilitate the expansion and modernization of the rail system.[91]

However, while these changes will shift the burden of subsidizing grain shipments out of Western Canada from the railways and other users of the rail system to the general taxpayer and should result in a significant upgrading of the rail network, this initiative is unlikely to alleviate any of the distortion in the western agricultural economy cause by the "Crow Rate." Net increases in the transportation rates paid by grain producers will be phased-in very gradually over the next eight years and will only amount to 60 percent of the actual cost of shipping grain by 1991/92. As a result, grain producers will continue to enjoy a 40 percent transportation subsidy which should provide western farmers with ample incentives to continue engaging in monoculture grain production rather than adopting cultivation and crop rotation practices that are less harmful to land productivity and soil conditions. Farmgate prices for feed grains will also remain significantly higher than would otherwise be the case, which will continue to constrain the diversification of western agriculture. Thus, the expansion of the monoculture grains economy in Western Canada will very likely continue for some time to come.

Pipelines and electrical transmission lines are the key transportation systems in the energy sector. While extensive networks of pipelines and transmission lines exist today, we can expect these networks to extend further into Canada's frontier regions in the future to tap the energy potential of the North and the offshore. We can also expect that, in the oil and gas sector, pipelines will be complemented by tankers, since it is argued that lower threshold reserves can be developed economically and earlier, using tankers as opposed to pipelines; 300–400 million barrels versus 2.5 billion barrels.[92] Tankers of course generate different environmental concerns.

e) Summary Conclusion

While the overall share of real output from resource-based industries has declined in the last twenty years, resource related activities still dominate the goods producing sector over secondary manufacturing. The service sector grew at a rapid rate in the post-war period in terms of employment, but not in terms of productivity. Since new technologies, particularly those related to information processing, will improve the productivity of the service sector, it is unlikely that this sector will continue to absorb workers at the same rates as in the past. However the tourism component of the service sector holds good potential for job-creation, if a major effort is made to develop Canada's tourism industry.

In the resource sector, agriculture and forestry are meeting resource base limitations, while fishery, mining and energy related activities are facing adverse international conditions. It is important to meet the emerging problems head-on, because a strong resource sector will be needed in the medium-term for balance of payments (B.O.P.) reasons. It is hoped, in the longer term, stresses on the resource sector will be alleviated by a stronger contribution to our B.O.P. by the manufacturing sector.

Related to the resource sector is the need to maintain a viable transportation infrastructure. Recent government policy proposals are aimed at modernizing and upgrading the rail systems. The policy will continue to encourage the expansion of the grain based economy in the West.

References

21. Primary manufacturing industries include food and beverages, tobacco products, wood industries, paper and allied products, primary metals, non-metallic minerals, and petroleum and coal products.
22. See Bruce Wilkinson, *Canada in the Changing World Economy*, C.D. Howe Research Institute, Montreal, 1980, pp.60-62.
23. John Britton and James Gilmour, *The Weakest Link: A Technological Perspective on Canadian Industrial Underdevelopment*. Background Study No. 43, Science Council of Canada, Ottawa, 1978, pp.39-40.
24. Wilkinson, op. cit.
25. See Appendix IV.
26. Ross Perry, *The Future of Canada's Auto Industry*, Canadian Institute for Economic Policy, Ottawa, 1982.
27. UK Ranga Chand, *The Growth of the Service Sector on the Canadian Economy*, unpublished manuscript, Ministry of State for Science and Technology, Ottawa, March 1982.
28. John A. Powell, Chairman, Tourism Sector, Consultative Task Force, *Report of the Tourism Sector Consultative Task Force*, Industry, Trade & Commerce, Ottawa, July 1978.
29. ibid.
30. ibid.
31. Tourism Consultative Task Force, op. cit.
32. Minister of Agriculture, July 1981.
33. Minister of Agriculture, op. cit.
34. D.R. Coote et al, *An Assessment of the Degradation of Agricultural Lands in Canada*, Agriculture Canada, Ottawa, 1981, pp.45-47.
35. Minister of Agriculture, op. cit.
36. Coote et al, op. cit, p.36.
37. Coote et al, p.21.
38. The Honourable John Roberts, Minister of the Environment, *A Forestry Sector Strategy for Canada*, Cabinet Discussion Paper, Environment Canada, Ottawa, September 1981, p.2.
39. The Honourable John Roberts, op. cit. p.2.
40. The Honourable John Roberts, op. cit. p.10.

41. Natural Forest Regeneration Conference, Quebec City, October 19-21, 1977, F.L.C. Reed, "Forest Management in Canada and Its Promise for the Future," in *Tomorrow's Forest . . . Today's Challenge*, Canadian Forestry Association, Ottawa, 1978.
42. The Honourable John Roberts, op. cit. p.11.
43. National Forest Regeneration Conference, op. cit. p.162.
44. The Honourable John Roberts, op. cit. p.11.
45. National Forest Regeneration Conference, op. cit. p.163.
46. The Honourable John Roberts, op. cit. p.10.
47. F.L.C. Reed and Associates, *Forestry Management in Canada*, Canadian Forestry Source, Environment Canada, January 1978, Volume 1.
48. The Honourable John Roberts, op. cit. p.15.
49. National Forestry Regeneration Conference, op. cit. p.172.
50. The Honourable John Roberts, op. cit. p.14.
51. Statistics Canada, *Summary of External Trade*, cat @ 65-001, December 1982.
52. Canada, Commission on Pacific Fisheries Policy, *Turning the Trade: A New Policy for Canada's Pacific Fisheries*, Supply and Services Canada, Vancouver, September 1982.
53. Ibid, p.9.
54. ibid, p.37.
55. Task Force on Atlantic Fisheries, *Navigating Troubled Waters: A New Policy for the Atlantic Fisheries*, Supply and Services Canada, Ottawa, December 1982, p.9.
56. ibid, p.38.
57. ibid, p.104.
58. ibid, p.103.
59. ibid, p.38.
60. ibid, p.50.
61. ibid, p.112.
62. ibid, p.50.
63. Energy, Mines and Resources Canada, *Mineral Policy: A Discussion Paper*, Supply and Services Canada, Ottawa, Dec. 1981, p.iii.
64. Statistics Canada, *Summary of External Trade*, cat. 65-001, Supply and Services Canada, Ottawa, Dec. 1982.
65. Energy, Mines and Resources Canada, op. cit. p.21.
66. ibid, pp.43-46.
67. ibid. p.37.
68. Energy, Mines and Resources Canada, The National Energy Program: Update, 1982, Supply and Services Canada, Ottawa, 1982, p.7.
69. Energy, Mines and Resources, op. cit., p.73.
70. ibid, p.137.
71. ibid, p.138.
72. ibid, p.139.
73. ibid, p.147.
74. ibid. p.100.
75. Canada, Report of the Special Committee on Alternative Energy and Oil Substitution to the Parliament of Canada, *Energy Alternatives*, Supply and Services Canada, Ottawa, 1981, p.37.

76. Energy, Mines and Resources Canada, *The National Energy Program: Update 1982*, Supply and Services Canada, 1982, p.13.
77. ibid, pp.82-83.
78. ibid, p.14.
79. ibid, p.41.
80. ibid, p.42.
81. Report of the Special Committee on Alternative Energy and Oil Substitution to the Parliament of Canada, op. cit. p.32.
82. National Energy Board, *Reasons for Decisions in the Matter of Phase II and Phase III of the Gas Export Omnibus Hearings, 1982*, Supply and Services Canada, Ottawa, Jan. 1983, pp.13-33.
83. ibid, p.24.
84. ibid, p.70.
85. Energy, Mines and Resources Canada, op. cit. p.64.
86. Energy, Mines and Resources Canada, *Mineral Policy: A Discussion Paper*, Supply and Services Canada, Ottawa, December 1981, p.9.
87. The Honourable John Roberts, op. cit., p.23.
88. Based on information available from Transport Canada.
89. Transport Canada.
90. Transport Canada.
91. Government of Canada, *Western Transportation Initiatives: The Policy Decision*, Transport Canada, Ottawa, February 1983.
92. Dome Petroleum Ltd.; Submission to the Special Committee of the Senate on the Northern Pipeline 1982.

6. Regional Perspectives

At a time when governments around the world are strengthening their executive branches so as to respond more effectively to the changing international order, the focus of power in Canada is shifting from the Federal to the Provincial governments.

The Canadian federal system has had to manage the persistent conflicts between the interests of the central industrialized provinces of Ontario and Quebec and those of the other regions, whose economies are based mainly on the export of staples. The weakening of the national economy in general and the combination of cultural and regional demands have strengthened the provinces in comparison to the central government.

The nature of Canada's economic development is intimately linked with the reconciliation of divergent regional economic interests. The BNA Act gave the Federal government control over the means to ensure the functioning of the economy (e.g., transportation, trade, money, banking, credit) and thus the ability to forge a strong national economy out of the scattered elements of British North America. The implementation of the National Policy soon after Confederation (with high tariffs to encourage local industries) ensured the dominance of central Canada over the rest of the country.

However, despite the bias given to centralization by the BNA Act and the general trend towards centralization in advanced industrialized countries, Canada moved, over time, to a more decentralized federalism.

Decentralization has a number of origins, including:

- a series of constitutional interpretations imposed upon the BNA Act by the Judicial Committee of the Privy Council in London in the latter half of the 19th century, which curtailed the power of the central government and greatly expanded the jurisdictional responsibilities of the provinces;

- the fact that the boundaries of the provinces were made coterminous with distinct economic regions and/or cultural groupings, thus ensuring that the provinces presented from their very beginning relatively coherent political interests;

- the fact that title to natural resources remained with the provinces. The development of resource-based economies weakened over time East-West trading links and reinforced a strong North-South pull as most of the resources came to be developed by American firms to service the American market;

91

- a weakened resolve to sustain a national economic system because of increasing American ownership of the industries of central Canada as well as those in the resources hinterland. Unique levels of foreign ownership (see Figure 6-1) undermined the role of the Canadian government vis-à-vis industry (e.g., export promotion, R&D support, etc.) since the objectives of the foreign-owned firms were not necessarily in keeping with the goals of a national economic policy.

Keynesian demand management policies in the immediate post-war period, designed to attain full employment, were principally concerned with aggregate demand management and not with the structure of the economy. Thus massive foreign direct investment in manufacturing, which eroded the power base of central Canada, was not perceived as an issue and the encouragement of natural resource exploitation, as a quick and easy way to maintain full employment, furthered the development of regional economies. Conflicts between the centre and the periphery were aggravated and the federal government was perceived as the defender of central Canada.

Figure 6-1
Degree of US Economic Control over Some Countries, 1970

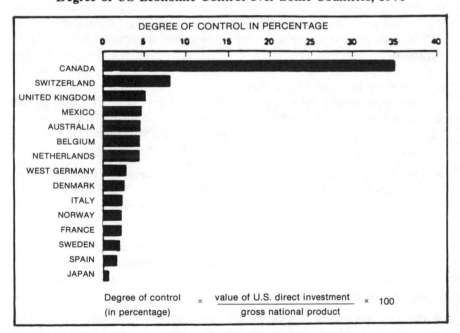

Source: Adapted from, Office de planification et du développement du Québec, *Valeurs et idéologies post-industrielles au Québec.* (dossier technique) tome 1, l'Editeur officiel du Québec, Québec, 1978, p.99.

Figure 6-2
Percentage of Value-Added and Employment by Industrial Activity
Canada 1975

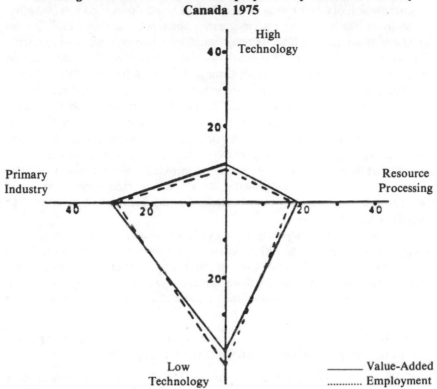

INDUSTRIAL STRUCTURE CATEGORIES

- **PRIMARY INDUSTRY**
  Agriculture
  Fishing
  Forestry
  Mining

- **LOW TECHNOLOGY**
  Food and Beverages
  Tobacco
  Labour-Intensive
    Secondary Processing
    (textiles, footwear,
    furniture, etc.)
  Metal Fabricating
  Transportation (excluding
    aircraft and parts)
  Electrical (excluding
    major appliances,

  communications, and
  industrial equipment)

- **RESOURCE PROCESSING**
  Wood Products
  Paper and Allied
  Primary Metal
  Non-Metallic Minerals
  Petroleum and Coal

- **HIGH TECHNOLOGY**
  Aircraft and Parts
  Electrical (major appliances,
    communications and
    industrial equipment)
  Chemicals and Chemical Products
  Miscellaneous Scientific
    and Professional Equipment

a) Regional Economies

The distinctiveness of Canada's regional economies is best illustrated by the distribution of interprovincial and foreign trade flows.[94] As can be appreciated from Table 6-1, no province other than B.C., Ontario and Quebec maintains more than half of its trade within its own provincial boundaries. Moreover, a majority of the provinces (including the Territories) at the periphery, have more trade outside Canada than with the rest of the country.

The pattern becomes even more evident when the distribution of trade movements in resources is analyzed. As can be seen from Table 6-2, only Ontario and Quebec maintain more than half their resource trade within their respective boundaries. This suggests that there is more potential for downstream processing in these two provinces than in the other provinces, which must export their resources. This perceived imbalance has led some provinces to develop economic policies aimed at developing new industries based upon their resource endowment. Both Tables 6-1 and 6-2 indicate how dependent Canada is on international trade.

Canada's resource dependence is also illustrated in Figure 6-2, 6-3, which sets out the country's industrial structure. Canada's overall "value added" and employment are concentrated in sectors with established technology, weighted toward primary resource extraction and low technology processing and manufacturing. Regionally, the industrial structure breaks down as follows:

- The *West* is heavily dependent on primary resource extraction (e.g. agriculture, energy) with comparatively little resource processing;

- *Ontario* and *Quebec* have similar industrial structures based on secondary manufacturing and the processing of resources. Both economies exhibit a dependence on relatively low-technology industries;

- *Atlantic* Canada is dependent on resources exploitation (e.g., fishing and forestry) with some preliminary resource processing.

The industrial structure reflects the nation's development and the traditional comparative advantages of particular regions.

b) Regional Aspirations

The regions have continually complained about federal economic policies, which they perceived as favouring central Canada at the expense of diversified industrial development throughout the country. For example, many Westerners have referred to the adverse effect of the low Crow's Nest Freight Rate, established in 1897, on the western agricultural sector; the low freight rates favoured grain exports at the expense of local feed grain usage, livestock production, growth of other crops and agricultural processing.[95] And in the same way that the periphery wants to redress economic imbalances

TABLE 6-1

Distribution of Interprovincial and Foreign Merchandise Trade, 1974

(low percentages)

Province	(1) Within Province	(2) Within Region[1]	(3) Rest of Canada	(4) 2 + 3	(5) Exports Abroad	(6) Total
Newfoundland	23 4	0.9	7.2	(8.1)	68.6	100.0
P.E.I.	45 4	18.9	27.0	(45.9)	8.7	100.0
Nova Scotia	44 8	11.6	19.4	(31.0)	24.2	100.0
New Brunswick	38 3	8.6	19.3	(27.9)	33.8	100.0
Quebec	53 6	—	28.3	—	18.2	100.0
Ontario	54 1	—	22.8	—	23.1	100.0
Manitoba	46 0	10.7	1.5	(32.2)	22.0	100.0
Saskatchewan	22 9	11.5	17.1	(28.6)	48.5	100.0
Alberta	38 5	13.7	16.5	(30.2)	31.2	100.0
British Columbia	52 7	6.3	4.4	(10.7)	36.5	100.0
Yukon/N.W.T.	7 1	10.4	6.7	(17.1)	75.8	100.0

Note: 1. Regional trade for Atlantic region includes the four Atlantic provinces and for the western region the four western provinces plus the Yukon and N.W.T.

Source: Statistics Canada, Unpublished Data (ref. 94).

TABLE 6-2
Distribution of Interprovincial and Foreign Trade in
Unprocessed Materials and Primary Manufactured Goods, 1974
(percentages)

Province	(1) Within Province	(2) Within Region	(3) Rest of Canada	(4) 2 + 3	(5) Exports Abroad	(6) Total	(7) Primary Goods as % of Province's Total Shipments	(8) % of All Canadian Primary Goods Shipments
Newfoundland	20.2	0.2	3.6	(3.8)	76.0	100	67.2	1.6
P.E.I.	43.5	18.2	28.9	(47.1)	9.3	100	89.1	0.3
Nova Scotia	42.5	8.2	16.7	(24.9)	32.6	100	50.3	2.0
New Brunswick	32.1	5.5	20.9	(26.4)	41.4	100	73.3	2.8
Quebec	54.7	—	20.0	—	25.3	100	44.7	22.0
Ontario	65.2	—	17.0	—	17.7	100	37.5	33.7
Manitoba	43.7	6.3	24.0	(30.3)	26.0	100	65.5	4.6
Saskatchewan	18.2	10.6	19.7	(30.3)	51.5	100	84.7	6.8
Alberta	30.1	12.7	20.0	(32.7)	37.3	100	69.0	11.0
British Columbia	42.7	5.4	4.7	(10.1)	47.2	100	75.3	14.8
Yukon/N.W.T.	2.6	11.0	7.1	(18.1)	79.9	100	94.1	0.5
								100.0

Source: Statistics Canada, unpublished data (ref. 94).

with central Canada, Quebec is intent on redressing perceived imbalances with Ontario. Provincial governments have begun to articulate industrial policies in their territories, that reflect their socio-economic aspirations. An example of those aspirations for Western Canada is shown in Figure 6-4. In the West however, one limit to industrial development could be the limited water supply in the Prairies.[96]

Figure 6-3
Percentage of Value-added and Employment by Industrial Activity
in Canadian Regions
1975

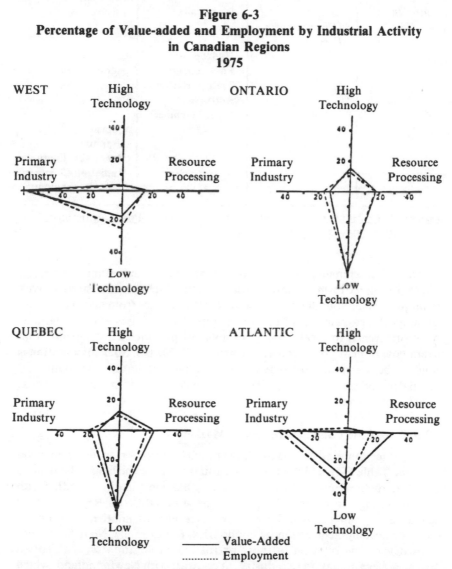

Value-Added
Employment

Source: DREE: Major Development Opportunities and Issues in Canada's Regions 1979.

Figure 6-4
Western High Technology Opportunity Matrix

Alberta	British Columbia	Manitoba	Saskatchewan
Fossil Fuels Petrochemicals Medicine	Fossil Fuels		Life Sciences (Biotechnology)
Electronics	Electronics Ocean Sciences Forestry	Electronics	Electronics
		Hydropower Food Sciences Transportation Aerospace Light Machinery	Agribusiness
			Potash Uranium Renewable Energy Radiation Chemistry and Technology

Source: R. Quittenton; Presentation at the Financial Post Conference, Oct. 19th, 20th, 1982, Regina, Sask.

One characteristic, common to all provincial industrial policies, is reliance on direct forms of intervention to stimulate new industrial activity within provincial boundaries. This intervention ranges from accepted financial support programs to direct ownership of enterprises and regulations, giving preference to local firms. Examples of provincial instruments, that govern government procurement, are listed in Table 6-3. Such intervention is found to be warranted because of the perceived limitations of traditional federal demand management policies to solve deep-rooted structural issues at the provincial level.

c) Erosion of the Canadian Common Market

Province-building has led to a large number of barriers to interprovincial trade (see Table 6-4), which have created many inefficiencies and distortions in the Canadian economy. Province-building has come in direct conflict with nation-building as provinces compete for the same industries. Regulations, or their absence, can be used by one province against another to promote economic development within its boundaries. For example, Nova Scotia has imposed very few rules on offshore petroleum exploration on the Scotian Shelf as a clear invitation to industry, in contrast with Newfoundland, which has a set of stringent regulations aimed at controlling the pace of development

Table 6-3
Provincial Government Procurement Policies

NEWFOUNDLAND: (a)
  —15% price premium for local suppliers, plus benefit/cost analysis (local preferred when benefit is 1.5 times added cost)
  —sourcing of both labour and materials
  —4-tier preference policy on consulting contracts (e.g. by location of office in province)
  —overall Canadian preference

PRINCE EDWARD ISLAND: (b)
  —no stated local preference policy
  —some informal preferences on local supplies

NOVA SCOTIA:
  —up to 10% price premium, applied selectively to specific local industries (c)
  —general local preference applied on smaller contracts (d)
  —restricted to local suppliers, if 3 or more available, or in other selected circumstances (c)

NEW BRUNSWICK: (c)
  —since October 1977 evaluates tenders by both cost and local benefit
  —includes subcontracting sources
  —restricted to local suppliers, if 3 or more available
  —some development of local source through "cost plus" contracting and product development assistance

MARITIME PROVINCES: (e)
  —Council of Maritime Premiers, March 12, 1980 announced changes in purchasing policy of New Brunswick, Nova Scotia and PEI to include "regional" value added in criteria for awarding contracts and purchase of materials
  —regional component not used if provincial supplier competitive
  —informally, 5-10% premium accepted before contracts granted to out-of-region firms

QUEBEC
  —10% price premium on contracts exceeding $50,000 (c)
  —in some circumstances (related to amount of competition within Quebec) restricted to local bids (d)

continued on page 100

—restrictions also used for provincial industrial development objectives

—local and Canadian content must be specified; this includes sub-contracts

ONTARIO:
—10% price premium to Canadian suppliers, also applied to all provincially funded agencies and industries receiving provincial assistance as of November 1980

—preference to Ontario firms only when bids competitive (d,f)

MANITOBA:
—preference only if price, delivery, quality equal (d)

ALBERTA:
—no local preference in purchasing of supplies, some large contracts (e.g. tourism programs) let only to Alberta firms

—on natural resource exploration and extraction permits and leases, firms allowed to tender restricted to those licenced to do business in Alberta

—bidders on certain major projects (tar sands, pipelines) must specify local employment, purchasing (g)

BRITISH COLUMBIA:
—10% price premium
—"committed" to provincial preference
—may use regional or sectoral unemployment, general health of industry as procurement criteria (c,d)

Sources:
(a) Government of Newfoundland, Department of Industrial Development
(b) Interview with PEI official
(c) Government of Canada, *Powers over the Economy: Securing the Canadian Economic Union in the Constitution*, CCMC, (Doc: 830-81/036), July 1980, pp. 29-31.
(d) J. Maxwell and C. Pestieau, *Economic Realities of Contemporary Confederation*, (Montreal, HRI, 1980, p. 87).
(e) Council of Maritime Premiers, "Regional Preference in Provincial Purchasing and Tendering Policies," Press Release, March 1980.
(f) F.S. Miler, *Supplementary Measures to Stimulate the Ontario Economy* (Government of Ontario, Nov. 1980).
(g) Interview with officials, Government of Alberta.

Table 6-4
Areas of Actual or Potential Provincial Impediments
to a Canadian Common Market

Trade

Procurement practices: Provincial governments may establish preferential treatment of goods produced within their provinces or of goods having a high provincial content. Such policies often extend to construction contracts and may cover purchases of professional services.

Marketing boards: In 1972 there were about 172 provincial farm marketing boards representing the sales of about one-quarter of total Canadian farm products.* These boards set production quotas and establish prices.

Liquor-buying practices: A variety of liquor-buying practices are used to give preference to provincial producers. These include pricing preferences and quota systems. Packaging regulations, such as Quebec's requirement that cider not be sold in containers used for beer, may discourage producers in other provinces.

Uniformity of legislation: The absence of a uniform code of commercial practice, for example, may raise the costs of doing business. As of 1976 three provinces had comprehensive unfair trade practice acts. In 1977, Saskatchewan passed a Consumer Products Warranties Act which differed from its counterpart in Ontario.

Transportation: Regulation of trucking, which is delegated to the provinces by the federal government, can create barriers to the free movement of goods. Some regional reciprocity is contributing to breaking down differentials in weights limits, bills of lading, licensing, maximum vehicle dimensions, and fuel taxes.

Labeling regulation and different product standards. These may serve as barriers to the free movement of goods.

Labor

Professional licensing: Professional certification, originally instituted to protect the public, may hamper labor mobility.

Apprenticeship and tradesmen's qualifications: Each province has its own regulations, although most of the provinces have attempted to agree upon interprovincial certification procedures.

Residence requirements for construction workers: These requirements have been a source of interprovincial tension, particularly in the recent dispute between Quebec and Ontario. Alberta stipulates that

continued on page 102

resource development projects should use provincial workers wherever practical.**

Public service standards: The scrapping of the federal Social Services Act in 1977 and the subsequent switch to an unconditional cash transfer system mean the abandonment of a commitment to a single national standard for such public services as rehabilitation of, and support for, the handicapped, protective and developmental services for children, and support services for the aged.

Students: University quotas and fee differentials may influence the mobility of students.

Service industries: Barriers to the interprovincial movement of services are not prohibited by the BNA Act.

Capital

Regulation of securities and prospectus requirements: These are regulated by the individual provinces, with some loose co-ordination among major stock exchanges. This may be a barrier to raising capital across provincial boundaries.

Competition policy: Provincial legislation covering corporation and securities does not significantly hinder interprovincial sales of corporate assets or takeover bids. Interjurisdictional statutory amalgamations are, however, hindered in some situations and barred in others, which creates a bias in favor of other methods of merging. There have been recent cases of provincial interference in takeover bids.

Pension plans: The requirement of the Canada Pension Plan that proceeds be invested in each province in proportion to the funds raised in it can be considered a barrier to the movement of capital. Quebec has a similar policy for its own pension plan.

Land: Several provinces have legislation banning non-residents from buying recreational or agricultural land.

Provincial investment plans: Several new plans are explained in more detail in Table 14.

Cultural

Language requirements: Requirements within individual provinces may establish barriers to trade and to labor mobility; they also create problems for such service industries as advertising and publishing.

Education and communications: Education falls under provincial jurisdiction, while communications are in the federal domain. Where

continued on page 103

the two overlap, as in the case of educational television, problems may arise.

Communications: All telephone companies are now federally regulated. British Columbia would like to regain regulatory jurisdiction over its telephone company.

* *Globe and Mail* (Toronto), February 3, 1977.

** According to the Alberta Department of Energy and Natural Resources.

Source: Maxwell J. and Pestieau; "Economic Realities of Contemporary Confederation," C.D. Howe Research Institute 1980, pp.88-89.

off its shore.[97] In this way provinces are able to effect structural changes in their respective economies.

This is very different from the original intent of Canadian federalism of keeping an internal common market as essential for the stimulation of international trade. To that end the federal government instituted a policy to reduce regional disparities, based on four distinct thrusts:

- income transfers to individuals to raise their living standards;

- programs to encourage industrial location in poorer regions;

- programs to ensure that public services are available up to a minimum national standard; and

- income transfers to provincial governments to help them maintain tax rates close to the national average.

While such activities run counter to economic efficiency, it was felt that a level of effectiveness could be attained in which all provinces participated in sustaining the economic union with minimal friction.

However, the problems of regional disparities have persisted and provincial governments became increasingly intent on developing their own economic strategies. This was officially recognized by the federal government in January 1982 with the amalgamation of the Department of Industry, Trade and Commerce (ITC) with the Department of Regional Economic Expansion (DREE) into the Department of Regional Industrial Expansion (DRIE). This action reflected two realities; the first was that the regions had differing industrial structures, which required different policies and the other was the inability of DREE to make a significant impact on the problem of regional disparity.

In this way the federal government hoped to rectify certain economic imbalances and maintain some semblance of economic union in the years ahead. The extent to which regional economic policies can be harmonized will relieve stresses on the resource base and the environment. However, as owners of their natural resources, the provinces can set regulations regarding the development of these resources and incentives to influence the location of industry. Use of these instruments to any significant extent would certainly create a variety of political, social and environmental stresses. The temptation will be increasingly great to use instruments that promote "province-building."

References

94. For detailed analysis see M. Jenkin, The Challenge of Diversity; Science Council of Canada (1984).
95. On February 1st 1983, the Federal Government announced changes to this policy that are aimed at rectifying some of the historical distortions in Western agriculture.
96. Foster H. D. and Sewell D.: op. cit.
97. See Voyer R: Offshore Oil; Canadian Institute for Economic Policy (1983).

7. Demographic Perspectives

An appreciation of demographic trends is basic to any analysis of the make-up of an economy, because they reveal a number of structural issues that require a long lead-time to correct since population characteristics change only gradually over time.

The link between population and economic development is now well recognized and has been studied since Malthus concluded in 1798 that the need for human sustenance provided the only check on population growth. Although the Industrial Revolution has upset the Malthusian scenario, policy makers have increasingly considered demographic trends in decision-making, because of their far reaching impacts in such diverse areas as health care, education, welfare, housing, labour, consumption, savings, not to mention voting behaviour. These are the kinds of considerations that are addressed in this chapter.

a) Future Demographic Patterns: An Overview

The Canadian population is expected to grow from about 24 million today to between 26.7 and 29.7 million by the year 2001[98] (see Table 7-1).

Most recent projections fall within these boundaries. The spread of 3 million people in the various scenarios is the result of cumulative effects due to different assumptions regarding fertility and mortality rates, immigration, emigration as well as internal migration, with fertility playing a particularly sensitive role (see Table 7-2). The population growth rate is expected to be about 1% in the 1980s and then fall below 1% in the 1990s. This growth pattern is generally reflected in each province with Alberta and B.C. expected to grow much more rapidly than average, while growth in Quebec and Manitoba is expected to be well below average (see Tables 7-3, 7-4).

Canada officially entered the club of aging nations with the 1971 Census (i.e. 8% of the population over 65 according to the U.N.). Canada will continue to have an increasingly aging population where, by 2001, some 3.5 million people will be over 65, up from 2.2 million in 1979. In addition, women are expected to predominate this group, because of the difference in the life expectancy between males and females. The sex ratio for the 65(+) age group

105

TABLE 7-1

Alternative Population Futures and Growth for Canada, 1981-2051

Projection Number[a]	Population (000's)					Growth (Average Annual Per Cent)		
	1981[b]	1991[b]	2001[b]	2051[b]	1981-91	1991-2001	2001-2051
1	24,187.3	26,748.0	28,480.7	28,931.9	1.01	0.63	0.03
2	24,187.3	26,802.5	28,622.5	29,367.9	1.03	0.66	0.05
3	24,180.4	26,501.0	27,851.1	25,041.5	0.92	0.50	-0.21
4	24,188.1	26,988.2	29,535.4	38,699.6	1.10	0.91	0.54
5	24,104.8	26,210.8	27,449.3	25,360.6	0.84	0.46	-0.16
6	24,187.3	26,743.0	28,463.6	28,720.3	1.01	0.63	0.02
7	24,187.3	26,749.8	28,486.5	29,014.2	1.01	0.63	0.04
8	24,188.1	27,043.0	29,679.2	39,202.5	1.12	0.93	0.56
9	24,098.0	25,968.6	26,838.8	21,732.7	0.75	0.33	-0.43
10	24,188.1	27,044.5	29,683.4	39,276.5	1.12	0.94	0.56
11	24,098.0	25,969.9	26,842.5	21,776.5	0.75	0.33	-0.42
12	24,187.3	26,749.0	28,484.0	28,977.8	1.01	0.63	0.03
13	24,187.3	26,748.8	28,483.2	28,968.3	1.01	0.63	0.03
14	24,053.1	25,865.1	26,783.6	22,985.7	0.73	0.35	-0.31

Notes: [a] See Table 6-2 for a brief description
   [b] As at June 1

Source: Foot D. op. cit.

TABLE 7-2
Summary of Assumptions Underlying the Population
Projections for Canada and the Provinces

Projection Number and Description	Fertility Rate for Canada[a]	Life Expectancy for Canada	Net Int'l. Migration to Canada (000's)	Interprov. Migration Pattern (Period)
1 No change	1.75	A[b]	65	1976-79
2 Increasing life expectancy	1.75	B[c]	65	1976-79
3 Low fertility	1.55	A	65	1976-79
4 High fertility	2.25	A	65	1976-79
5 Low immigration	1.75	A	25	1976-79
6 "Return" interprov. migration	1.75	A	65	1976-75[d]
7 "Westward" inter-prov. migration	1.75	A	65	C[e]
8 High population	2.25	B	65	1976-79
9 Low population	1.55	A	25	1976-79
10 High population and "westward" migration	2.55	B	65	C
11 Low population and "westward" migration	1.55	A	25	C
12 In-migration sensitivity	1.75	A	65	C/1976-79[f]
13 Out-migration sensitivity	1.75	A	65	1976-79/C[f]
14 Zero net int'l migration	1.75	A	0	1976-79

Notes:
[a] Achieved by 2001.
[b] A - Increasing life expectancy based on 1971-76 trends
[c] B - Further increases in life expectancy beyond those incorporated into A.
[d] A partial reversal to the 1966-75 patterns by 1986-87.
[e] C - Continuation of the 1976-79 patterns with further westward shift.
[f] In-migration pattern/out-migration pattern.

Source: Foot D.: op. cit.

TABLE 7-3
Alternative Population Futures for Canada and the Provinces, 2001
(000's)

Projection Number	Can	Nfld	PEI	NS	NB	PQ	Ont	Man	Sask	Alta	BC	Yukon	NWT
1	28,480.7	678.9	154.0	1,007.3	850.4	6,338.0	10,196.1	1,087.6	1,218.7	3,300.7	3,578.2	22.6	48.2
2	28,622.5	682.3	154.4	1,011.6	853.9	6,362.7	10,259.2	1,093.7	1,226.3	3,317.2	3,590.1	22.7	48.5
3	27,851.1	650.4	149.3	985.6	831.4	6,220.9	10,007.6	1,060.1	1,173.9	3,201.5	3,504.1	21.7	44.7
4	29,535.4	695.0	158.6	1,045.8	882.6	6,590.1	10,597.6	1,123.5	1,248.7	3,410.7	3,711.1	23.3	48.6
5	27,449.3	669.8	150.7	987.6	834.2	6,169.2	9,728.8	1,047.3	1,189.7	3,175.3	3,428.1	21.8	46.7
6	28,463.6	677.2	148.7	987.7	826.3	6,626.4	10,545.8	1,168.7	1,012.9	2,833.1	3,546.9	29.9	60.0
7	28,486.5	643.7	143.4	943.8	796.9	6,228.3	9,835.1	1,110.0	1,218.8	3,642.2	3,863.0	19.6	41.7
8	29,679.2	698.3	159.0	1,050.1	886.2	6,615.0	10,661.5	1,129.7	1,256.4	3,427.5	3,723.2	23.4	48.9
9	26,838.8	641.6	146.1	966.3	815.6	6,054.9	9,547.7	1,020.7	1,145.9	3,079.2	3,356.6	21.0	43.3
10	29,683.4	662.0	148.0	983.6	830.2	6,499.9	10,282.5	1,153.2	1,256.5	3,783.3	4,021.8	20.3	42.3
11	26,842.5	608.5	136.1	905.7	764.6	5,950.0	9,205.2	1,042.0	1,146.0	3,401.6	3,627.1	18.2	37.4
12	28,484.0	660.0	147.5	966.1	815.7	6,285.4	10,003.5	1,096.0	1,220.7	3,489.3	3,734.5	20.9	44.4
13	28,483.2	662.6	149.9	985.0	831.5	6,281.4	10,028.4	1,102.3	1,217.7	3,451.7	3,706.1	21.2	45.5
14	26,783.6	674.5	149.0	982.0	829.0	6,260.8	9,362.4	990.1	1,163.6	2,995.3	3,310.4	21.5	45.2

Source: Foot D.: op. cit.

TABLE 7-4

Alternative Future Population Growth for Canada and the Provinces, 1981-2001

(Average Annual Per Cent)

Projection Number	Can	Nfld	PEI	NS	NB	PQ	Ont	Man	Sask	Alta	BC	Yukon	NWT
1	0.82	0.76	1.02	0.78	0.87	0.02	0.81	0.24	1.08	2.17	1.47	0.25	0.50
2	0.85	0.78	1.03	0.80	0.89	0.04	0.84	0.27	1.11	2.20	1.49	0.27	0.53
3	0.71	0.55	0.87	0.67	0.76	-0.08	0.71	0.11	0.89	2.02	1.37	0.06	0.13
4	1.00	0.88	1.17	0.97	1.06	0.21	1.00	0.40	1.20	2.34	1.66	0.40	0.54
5	0.65	0.70	0.92	0.68	0.78	-0.11	0.59	0.07	0.97	2.00	1.28	0.08	0.35
6	0.82	0.75	0.84	0.68	0.73	0.24	0.98	0.60	0.16	1.40	1.43	1.63	1.58
7	0.82	0.49	0.66	0.45	0.55	-0.07	0.63	0.34	1.08	2.67	1.86	-0.45	-0.22
8	1.03	0.90	1.18	0.99	1.08	0.23	1.03	0.43	1.23	2.37	1.68	0.43	0.57
9	0.54	0.48	0.76	0.58	0.67	-0.20	0.50	-0.06	0.78	1.84	1.18	-0.10	-0.02
10	1.03	0.63	0.82	0.66	0.75	0.14	0.85	0.53	1.23	2.87	2.07	-0.27	-0.15
11	0.54	0.22	0.41	0.25	0.35	-0.29	0.32	0.04	0.78	2.35	1.56	-0.80	-0.74
12	0.82	0.62	0.81	0.57	0.66	-0.02	0.71	0.28	1.09	2.45	1.69	-0.14	0.09
13	0.82	0.64	0.88	0.67	0.76	-0.03	0.72	0.31	1.08	2.40	1.65	-0.05	0.21
14	0.54	0.72	0.86	0.65	0.75	-0.04	0.42	-0.19	0.86	1.74	1.12	0.00	0.20

Source: Foot D.: op. cit.

drops from 0.75 males per female in 1981 to 0.66 in 2001, while in the population as a whole the sex ratio drops from 0.984 males per female in 1981 to 0.962 by 2001. This aging process means that with a declining population in the ages from 1 to 14, there will be relatively more people of working age (15 to 64 years) to the end of the century than ever experienced before in Canadian history.

Canada clearly faces the consequences of some inevitable demographic trends between now and the year 2001; a slowly growing, female-dominant, aging population with a large labour force. The implication of some of these developments are explored in the following sections.

b) Urbanization

The urbanization process, which began to accelerate in the early 1950s, is expected to continue and Canada's urban population[99] could include 90% of all Canadians by the year 2000, up from 75% today.[100] Some 32% of the population may be expected to live in Montreal, Toronto and Vancouver.

This rapidly increasing level of urbanization entails a number of consequences including the following:

- pressure on housing accommodation; particularly as related to lower income groups and to the older segments of the population;

- pressure on public services (e.g., transportation, health, law enforcement, waste treatment);

- encroachment on prime agricultural land;

- social unrest due to large scale unemployment (see Section C) and growing incidence of crime.[101]

Such stresses could be further exacerbated by the inability of cities to develop the revenue base to deal effectively with socio-economic and environmental problems caused by the process of urbanization and by associated industrial activities. Socio-economic and environmental indicators for selected Canadian cities are shown in Tables 7-5 to 7-8. Financial resource transfers to the level of the municipality will be needed to ease the strains of the urbanization process.

c) An Aging Society

Canadian society will continue its aging process until well into the 21st century. However, as can be noted from Figure 7-1, except for the Baby Boom of the 1950s, Canadian society has been aging for some time. Moreover, as can be seen from Figure 7-2 the decline of the young has been more rapid than the increase in the elderly. Therefore, there are relatively more people of working age in the population.

TABLE 7-5
Property crimes, traffic accidents and police statistics,[1] 1975-77[2]

| | Serious property crimes per 1,000 population | Traffic accidents | | Car accidents per 1,000 population | Police manpower per 1,000 population | Police vehicles per mile of public thoroughfare |
		Persons killed per 1,000 population	Persons injured per 1,000 population			
Toronto	12.9	0.05	7.4	20.9	1.94	0.17
Montreal	27.2	0.09	6.5	30.3	2.35	0.21
Vancouver	30.5	0.11	8.3	39.8	1.65	0.11
Ottawa	22.4	0.07	7.4	31.1	1.64	0.16
Winnipeg	23.3	0.87	11.6	53.4	1.80	0.07
Edmonton	32.6	0.10	4.4	36.1	1.78	0.09
Quebec	23.6	0.13	2.8	48.0	1.81	0.17
Hamilton	24.7	0.07	10.4	23.2	1.68	0.14
Calgary	24.5	0.10	2.5	37.8	1.89	0.22
Kitchener	15.3	0.10	8.9	27.2	1.49	0.07
London	17.2	0.07	11.9	31.9	1.40	0.13
Halifax	29.9	0.08	5.0	36.1	2.13	0.23
Windsor	20.1	0.11	11.4	26.3	1.91	0.10
Victoria	24.9	0.11	9.8	34.5	1.76	0.11
Sudbury	16.2	0.14	7.3	20.9	1.23	0.06
Regina	36.0	0.67	7.7	37.2	1.82	0.09
St. John's	22.0	0.06	5.0	37.3	2.45	0.18
Saskatoon	19.8	0.97	8.0	46.0	1.79	0.06
Saint John	19.1	0.14	7.7	29.8	2.31	0.08
Sherbrooke	24.1	0.10	2.0	44.2	1.78	0.10
Trois-Rivières	17.8	0.17	4.1	40.0	2.21	0.12
Kingston	23.1	0.07	7.8	24.3	1.80	0.18

[1] Figures are from data collected by individual municipal police forces. In some cases the area of jurisdiction may not correspond exactly to the boundaries of the Census Metropolitan Area. In these cases, however, the difference in the population involved is small.

[2] Calculations are based on three-year averages of crime traffic and police data.

Source: Crime and Traffic Enforcement Statistics, Catalogue 85-205: *Police Administration Statistics*, Catalogue 85-204. Justice Statistics Division, Statistics Canada, unpublished data.

TABLE 7-6
Air pollution indices

Urban area[5,6]	Actual suspended particulates level as a ratio of national maximum acceptable standards[1]			Sulphur dioxide level as a ratio of national maximum acceptable standards[2]		
	1974	1975	1976	1974	1975	1976
Toronto	1.16	1.01	0.90	0.60	0.75	0.75
Montreal	1.83	1.44	1.11	2.60	1.80	1.35
Vancouver	..	..	0.97	..	0.55	0.50
Ottawa	1.30	1.10	0.86	1.20	1.00	0.90
Winnipeg	..	1.07	1.14	..	<0.50	<1.00
Edmonton	1.01	1.67	1.96	<0.50	<0.50	<0.50
Quebec	1.49	1.47	1.21	..	..	1.20
Hamilton	1.50	1.40	1.44	1.10	1.00	1.05
Calgary	1.74	1.78	1.59	<0.50	<0.50	<0.50
London	1.31	1.04	0.91	<0.50	<0.50	<0.65
Halifax	0.67	0.74	0.49	..	0.90	0.65
Windsor	1.74	1.14	1.09	1.65	1.45	1.35
Victoria	0.63	0.63	0.66	<0.50	<0.50	..[3]
Sudbury	0.79	0.71	0.66	..	..	0.95
Regina	0.94	0.91	0.81	<0.50	<0.50	..
St. John's	0.73	0.70	0.71	..	..	..
Saskatoon	1.01	1.10	1.30	<0.50	<0.50	..
Saint John	0.86	0.79	0.79	1.25	0.70	..
Sherbrooke	..	..	0.77	..	..	..[4]
Trois-Rivières	..	..	1.03	..	..	1.10

[1]Particulates, annual geometric mean in micrograms per cubic metre divided by 70 micrograms per cubic metre. Figures over one indicate acceptable maximum is exceeded.

[2]Sulphur dioxide, annual geometric mean in parts per hundred million divided by 2.0 parts per hundred million. Figures over one indicate acceptable maximum is exceeded.

[3]In many cases where data is not available there was insufficient data for calculation of a valid average figure.

[4]No station measuring sulphur dioxide.

[5]Data are not available for Oshawa, Kitchener and Kingston.

[6]Readings were taken in the Central Area of cities.

Source: The Clean Air Act Annual Report, Environmental Protection Service, Environment Canada, 1976-77.

TABLE 7-7
Waste water and water supply treatment

Urban area[1]	Water supply treatment	Waste water treatment
	% of population served	
Toronto	98.5	95.1
Montreal	98.6	4.9
Vancouver	. .[2]	84.3
Ottawa	92.1	71.9
Winnipeg	100.0	100.0
Edmonton	100.0	100.0
Quebec	95.2	1.2
Hamilton	96.8	93.0
Calgary	100.0	100.0
Kitchener	98.0	98.0
London	100.0	100.0
Halifax	96.1	—
Windsor	98.2	87.5
Victoria	92.0	88.3
Sudbury	77.3	77.8
Regina	100.0	100.0
St. John's	87.9	1.0
Saskatoon	99.9	99.9
Saint John	91.7	29.6
Sherbrooke	91.8	5.8
Trois-Rivières	88.9	—
Kingston	85.2	78.9

[1]Does not include the rural fringe of the Census Metropolitan Areas and Census Agglomerations. In a number of cases data were not available for certain municipalities within the urban core and urban fringe, therefore necessary adjustments to the population totals were made.

[2]For the Vancouver CMA data on water supply treatment was not available for a large proportion of the area, therefore no figure is presented.

Source: National Inventory of Municipal Waterworks and Waste Water Systems in Canada, 1977. Department of Supply and Services, Ottawa, 1978.

TABLE 7-8
High Stressor industrial activity[1]

Urban areas[2]	Number of establishments in the high stressor group	Percentage of all establishments in the high stressor group	Number of workers in the high stressor group	Percentage of all industrial workers in the high stressor type	Fossil fuel purchased by high stressor industries	Percentage of fossil fuels purchased by high stressor industries
			000s			10^{12} Btus
Toronto	47	0.8	3.6	1.6	12.2	10.4
Montreal	52	1.0	7.2	3.5	20.3	31.9
Vancouver	38	2.0	2.5	4.6	8.2	45.1
Ottawa	17	4.7	4.3	31.5	10.9	86.5
Winnipeg	11	1.2	0.6	2.0	3.3	30.8
Edmonton	23	3.7	2.3	14.1	24.9	68.8
Quebec	9	1.8	1.7	9.5	7.2	76.6
Hamilton	15	2.3	21.3	40.2	29.2	67.8
Calgary	11	2.1	1.0	8.6	3.7	43.5
Kitchener	4	0.8	0.1	0.4	0.1	1.2
London	7	1.8	0.1	0.5	0.1	1.8
Halifax	7	4.9	0.3	1.1	0.1	5.7
Windsor	4	1.0	0.5	1.8	5.4	39.1
Victoria	6	2.9	0.1	2.5	0.1	20.0
Sudbury	8	11.3	5.0	88.4	25.5	98.4
Regina	7	5.1	0.3	8.8	1.5	48.4
St. John's	3	4.2	0.1	5.4	0.1	12.3
Saskatoon	5	3.7	0.2	4.9	0.3	20.0
Saint John	6	7.1	1.4	25.1	6.2	73.0

[1]In *Human Activity and the Environment*, industries were grouped into High Medium and Low Stressor categories depending on the impact these activities have, or could have on the environment. The high stressor group includes industries that deal with large scale bulk refining and concentration of raw materials. These industries typically require high energy inputs and may generate a significant volume of pollution.
[2]Data were not available for Kingston, Sherbrooke, Oshawa or Trois-Rivières.

The growing proportion of elderly and the decreasing proportion of young people suggests that financial and other support resources should be shifted from the latter to the former. Economies of scale are to be gained in the services provided to the elderly, while the reverse may create stresses on programs aimed at the young. This shift becomes of importance so as to ease the tax burden on the working-age population, because the per person total government expenditures are approximately 2½ times greater for the elderly than for the young.[102] The most obvious areas of transfer for resources are from education to health care and housing for the elderly.

d) A Growing Labour Force

As can be appreciated from Figure 7-3, Canada's labour force will continue to grow well into the next century. The implications are far-reaching given the high levels of unemployment that Canada is experiencing and the sluggish performance of the economy.

Figure 7-1
Historical and Future Median Age, Canada, 1851-2051

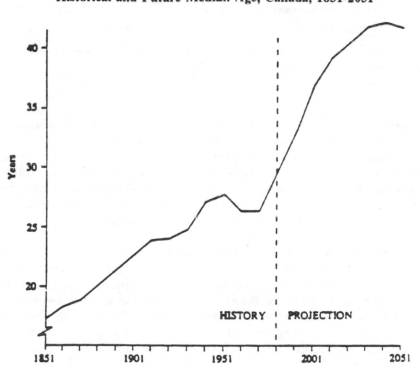

Source: Foot, op. cit.

Figure 7-2
Historical and Future Age Composition, Canada, 1851-2051

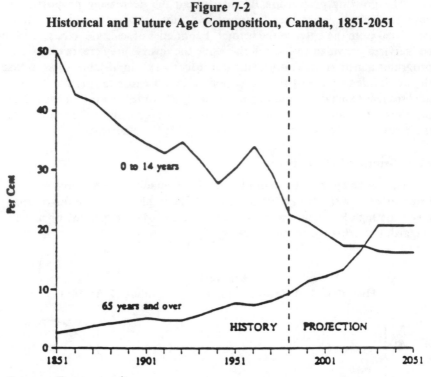

Source: Foot, op. cit.

Foot calculates, based on the projections of Figure 7-3, that to maintain the 1980 unemployment rate of 7.5% some 2.3 million new jobs would have to be generated in the 1980s.[103] This does not, on the surface, appear to be an impossible task since 2.75 million new jobs were created in the 1970s. However, in the 1970s, growth in real output (GNP) averaged 3.9% per annum. It is unlikely that similar levels of economic growth can be maintained in the 1980s, which means that unemployment will persist at very high levels, and well above Foot's calculations.

While the mainstream economic advice to government is to use the traditional demand management levers to stimulate the economy, some economists are beginning to comment on the structural nature of the unemployment problem and the limitations of traditional macro-economic levers in dealing with this issue. Recently Wassily Leontief described how his input-output model, as applied to the Austrian economy, revealed some of the underlying issues related to unemployment.[104] As he observed:

"The projections that carry the present state-of-the-art labour saving technology into full application everywhere in the Austrian economy by 1990 lead in all cases to the largest increase in gross

Figure 7-3
Historical and Alternative Labour Force Futures,
Canada, 1966-2051

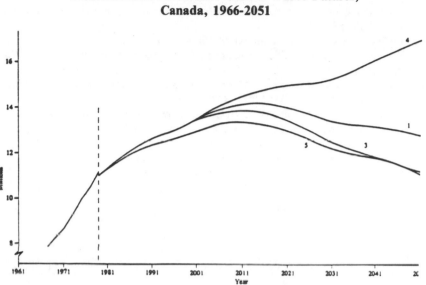

Note: Numbers refer to projection numbers. See Table 6-2.
Source: Foot, op. cit.

domestic product—but also to the highest levels of unemployment, to unemployment of 10 percent, a level not experienced in Austria since the dark days of the 1930s. With curtailment in the length of the work week at the maximum level of mechanization, the direction both the positive and negative changes remains the same but their absolute magnitudes are reduced. Unemployment in this case comes closer to the civilized Austrian experience of 2 percent."

Employment policies in the face of technological advances have to recognize the deep structural nature of the problem so that innovative solutions can be set in place.

e) In Sum

Demographic trends suggest a growing level of stress on Canadian society because financial and other support resources will have to be transferred to new areas, such as the support of the elderly, alleviation of unemployment and increased public services in urban areas. These transfers will not occur easily because people do not give up existing resources readily. However, these transfers will have to take place to alleviate the tax burden and to maintain an acceptable level of quality of life, particularly in our urban areas.

References

98. Foot D.: Canada's Population Outlook; Canadian Institute for Economic Policy, 1982.
99. Defined as cities greater than 100,000 inhabitants.
100. Science Council of Canada; Population, Technology and Resources, Report No. 25, July 1976.
101. Stone L.D. and Marceau C.: Canadian Population Trends and Public Policy Through the 1980s; IRPP 1977 p.41.
102. Canada Treasury Board Secretariat; "Changing Population and the Impact on Government Age-Specific Expenditures" Ottawa, 1977.
103. Foot, op. cit. p.212.
104. Leontief W.; Scientific American, Sept. 1982, p.188.

8. Institutional Perspectives

Government has always played an important role in fostering the development of Canada. In fact, a government strategy for economic development linking resources, railroads and manufacturers was essential to the creation of a separate country on the northern portion of the North American continent in the late 19th Century.

Government became involved in economic development, not only through the support of the private sector but also when necessary through direct involvement in partnership with the private sector and through public corporations. The result is a mixed economy with government size and influence growing steadily over the years. However, while large, government in Canada is not as large as in many other countries (see Table 8-3).

One principal reason for the growth of government has been the emergence of the "welfare state" in the post-war years, whereby government increasingly provided various forms of social assistance and social security to the point where the social affairs programs within the budgetary envelope are now by far the largest of the expenditure categories (i.e. — some 40% of the total budget) as can be appreciated from Table 8-1. These expenditures consist of transfer payments to the provinces including support for education, health care, old age security, guaranteed income supplement and so on. These expenditures reflect a social policy, which embraces both redistribution of income and "quality of life" objectives related to culture, health care, etc.

There is growing pressure to find new ways of supporting such programs to alleviate pressure on the federal budget.[105]

A strong political dimension underlies much economic decision-making in Canada, but then all important economic decisions are, in large part, political decisions. Big government, large corporations and large trade unions are the major institutional elements in our system of governance—a decision-making system, where what is being allocated is not only scarce economic resources but *power*. The role of some of these institutions is reviewed below.

a) Government and Economic Development

The Federal Government participates in economic development by setting the overall macro-economic framework through monetary and fiscal policy and participates at the micro-economic level both indirectly through various support programs and directly through public investment. Economic policy is set at Cabinet level and managed through the executive bureaucratic system. However, that system has much influence in setting economic directions.[106]

119

TABLE 8-1
The Federal Expenditure Plan by Envelope

	1980-81	1981-82	1982-83	1983-84	1984-85	1985-86
Economic development						
Millions of dollars	5,183	6.767	7,559	8.644	9,576	10,622
Percentage change	−3.5	30.6	11.7	14.4	10.8	10.9
Percentage of total	8.8	9.9	9.9	10.2	10.2	10.3
Energy						
Millions of dollars	3,624	2,672	3,039	3,602	4,115	4,779
Percentage change	53.4	−26.3	13.8	18.5	14.2	16.1
Percentage of total	6.2	3.9	4.0	4.2	4.4	4.6
Social Affairs						
Millions of dollars	24,633	27,693	30,150	33,795	37,571	41,683
Percentage change	8.6	12.4	8.9	12.1	11.2	10.9
Percentage of total	42.0	40.5	39.5	39.7	40.0	40.4
Justice and Legal						
Millions of dollars	1,213	1,399	1,541	1,750	1,930	2,133
Percentage change	17.0	15.3	10.2	13.6	10.3	10.5
Percentage of total	2.1	2.0	2.0	2.1	2.1	2.1
Services to Government						
Millions of dollars	2,732	3,350	3,448	3,676	3.852	4,213
Percentage change	17.0	22.6	2.9	6.6	4.8	9.4
Percentage of total	4.7	4.9	4.5	4.3	4.1	4.1
Parliament						
Millions of dollars	130	140	156	174	192	209
Percentage change	31.3	7.7	11.4	11.5	10.2	8.9
Percentage of total	0.2	0.2	0.2	0.2	0.2	0.2
Defence						
Millions of dollars	5,058	5,915	7,000	8,000	8,850	9,800
Percentage change	15.2	16.9	18.2	14.2	10.6	10.7
Percentage of total	8.6	8.7	9.2	9.4	9.4	9.5
External Affairs						
Millions of dollars	1,421	1,728	2,167	2,508	2,819	3,329
Percentage change	1.2	21.6	25.4	15.7	12.3	18.1
Percentage of total	2.4	2.5	2.8	2.9	3.0	3.2

TABLE 8-1 (cont'd)
The Federal Expenditure Plan by Envelope

	1980-81	1981-82	1982-83	1983-84	1984-85	1985-86
Fiscal Arrangements						
Millions of dollars	3,908	4,477	4,971	5,610	6,242	6,901
Percentage change	7.5	14.6	11.0	12.9	11.2	10.6
Percentage of total	6.7	6.6	6.5	6.6	6.6	6.7
Central Reserve						
Millions of dollars	0	500	800	900	1,050	1,150
Percentage change	—	—	60.0	12.5	16.7	9.5
Percentage of total	0	0.7	1.0	1.1	1.1	1.1
Lapse						
Millions of dollars	0	−1,035	−1,196	−1,424	−1,557	−1,694
Percentage change	—	—	15.6	19.1	9.3	8.8
Percentage of total	0	−1.5	−1.6	−1.7	−1.7	−1.6
General overhead reduction						
Millions of dollars	—	—	−100	−100	−100	−100
Total outlays (excluding public debt charges)						
Millions of dollars	47,902	53,605	59,535	67,135	74,540	83,025
Percentage change	10.6	11.9	11.1	12.8	11.0	11.4
Percentage of total	81.8	78.5	78.0	78.8	79.4	80.4
Public debt charges						
Millions of dollars	10,687	14,695	16,765	18,015	19,360	20,275
Percentage change	25.4	37.5	14.1	7.5	7.5	4.7
Percentage of total	18.1	21.5	22.0	21.2	20.6	19.6
Total outlays						
Millions of dollars	58,589	68,300	76,300	85,150	93,900	103,300
Percentage change	13.0	16.6	11.7	11.6	10.3	10.0
Percentage of total	100.0	100.0	100.0	100.0	100.0	100.0

Source: Canada. *The Budget in More Detail* (Ottawa: November 12, 1981).

Macro-economic Institutions

The first level of economic policy making takes place within those few government agencies responsible for macro-economic management; mainly The Bank of Canada, the Department of Finance and the Ministry of State for Economic and Regional Development (MSERD).

Responsibility for monetary policy rests with the Bank of Canada, which operates as an independent entity. While political control is maintained by Government, the Governor of the Bank must receive specific written directives from Government in cases where there is a difference of opinion concerning monetary policy.

In recent years the Bank of Canada has been heavily criticized for its high interest rate policy and its support of the Canadian dollar. The fact that the Bank of Canada followed, in a seemingly servile manner, US monetary policy, illustrates the limited freedom of action that Canada has vis-à-vis the US because the two economies are so closely intertwined. As the Economic Council observed in its 1982 Annual Review (p. 18): "In an effort to dampen fluctuations in the external value of the Canadian dollar, the Bank of Canada was left with little choice, but to let Canadian interest rates follow those in the United States."

This dependence on US policy has created a number of stresses: business failures, increased unemployment as well as the borrowing of some $7 billion (US) since 1975 to bolster the value of the Canadian dollar. Fiscal policy has been restrictive and supportive of monetary policy in recent years.

The lack of manoeuvering room at the macro-economic policy level has led Canadians to question the role of macro-economic institutions and to look increasingly to other institutions for directions for economic development. As noted in Chapter 5, provincial governments are playing an increasingly active role in economic affairs.

Public Sector Instruments at the Micro-economic Level

Micro-economic instruments are varied (e.g. — grants, regulations, special incentives, etc.). While a number of support programs are in place to encourage economic development through the private sector, Government (at the Federal and Provincial levels) has often had to intervene directly leading to an increased role of government in the economy. The reasons for state intervention are at least four-fold:

- *default:* the state was forced to concern itself with economic development as a result of the failure of private concerns (e.g., DEVCO, SYSCO, Canadair, etc.);

- *national security:* the state was forced to act in areas, where the national interest dictated such intervention (e.g., uranium mining and the setting up of Eldorado Nuclear; energy self-sufficiency and Petro-Canada);

- *development:* in many instances the state has to provide the foundation for development (e.g., utilities, transportation and other infra-structure costs) and to initiate development, when the private sector considered the risks too high (e.g., Panarctic Oil, SOQUIP, SOQUEM);

- *control:* where the market system did not provide for sufficient revenue to the state, continued welfare of workers (including cultural safeguards and sufficient domestic control over decisions on technological development), the state has had to intervene to ensure control over an activity (e.g., CBC, potash in Saskatchewan, asbestos in Quebec).

Canada is in fact a country, which practises state capitalism. While this may seem odd to many Canadians, because the dominant norms of economic behaviour come from the US, it is perfectly normal in a European sense, where state capitalism is also practised to overcome market failure. So Canada is not abnormal, but more like the rest of the world than like the US.

Some 400 federal and 250 provincial Crown Corporations, with specific mandates, have come into being over time.[107] Moreover, the rate of growth of provincial Crown Corporations was more rapid than that for their federal counterparts in the 1970s, reflecting the increased intervention of provincial governments in provincial economic development relative to the federal government.

The fact that there is a high level of public ownership in Canada indicates that a relatively high level of intervention is needed in Canadian public policy; the Canadian system is far removed from the ideal self-regulating system of classical economics as shown in Figure 8-1. Of course, this high degree of intervention leads to questions of accountability, which are often not easy to answer since the mandates of public sector institutions are usually broader and more diffuse than the narrower profit-orientation of the private sector. For example, Petro-Canada has the double mandate of acting as an instrument of state to be a "window on industry" as well as operating as a profit-oriented petroleum company.

However, to be effective, government has to share its power with business and labour.

b) The Corporate Sector and Economic Development

While accountability in the private sector appears on the surface to be a manageable problem, the issue can take on different dimensions, when firms get to a size where they can exert the power of a monopoly or oligopoly. The Canadian economic environment has permitted such firms to flourish and the issue of corporate concentration is continually on the political agenda.

Corporate aggregate concentration has increased in the post-war period (see Figure 8-2) to the point, where it is about twice that in the US (see Figure 8-3). The top Canadian firms are larger in relation to the Canadian economy

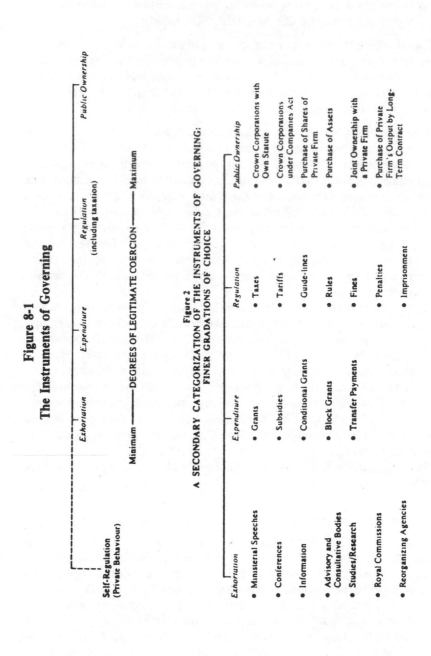

Figure 8-1
The Instruments of Governing

Exhortation	Expenditure	Regulation (including taxation)	Public Ownership

Minimum ——— DEGREES OF LEGITIMATE COERCION ——— Maximum

Self-Regulation
(Private Behaviour)

Figure 2
A SECONDARY CATEGORIZATION OF THE INSTRUMENTS OF GOVERNING: FINER GRADATIONS OF CHOICE

Exhortation	*Expenditure*	*Regulation*	*Public Ownership*
• Ministerial Speeches	• Grants	• Taxes	• Crown Corporations with Own Statute
• Conferences	• Subsidies	• Tariffs	• Crown Corporations under Companies Act
• Information	• Conditional Grants	• Guide-lines	• Purchase of Shares of Private Firm
• Advisory and Consultative Bodies	• Block Grants	• Rules	• Purchase of Assets
• Studies/Research	• Transfer Payments	• Fines	• Joint Ownership with a Private Firm
• Royal Commissions		• Penalties	• Purchase of Private Firm's Output by Long-Term Contract
• Reorganizing Agencies		• Imprisonment	

Source: Tupper and Doern, op. cit.

Figure 8-2

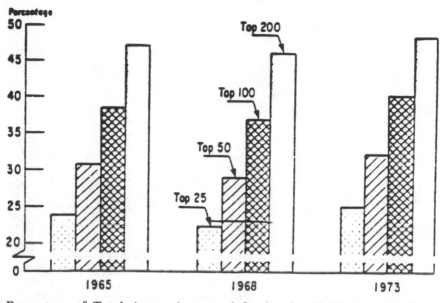

Percentage of Total Assets Accounted for by the 25-200 Largest* Non-Financial Corporations, Canada, 1965, 1968 and 1973.
Source: RCCC research.
Note: *Ranked by assets.

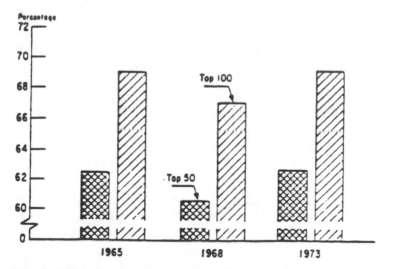

Percentage of Total Assets Accounted for by the 50 and 100 Largest* Financial Corporations, Canada, 1965, 1968 and 1973.
Source: RCCC research.
Note: *Ranked by assets.

Figure 8-3

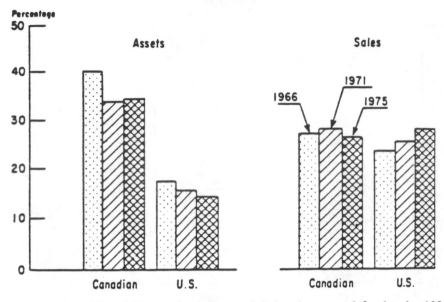

Percentage of Total Domestic Assets and Sales Accounted for by the 100
Largest* Non-Financial Corporations, Canada and the United States, 1966,
1971 and 1975.
Source: RCCC research.
Note: *Ranked by sales.

than are the top US firms in relation to the US economy. Students of
corporate concentration can only conclude that in the Canadian economy the
largest 100 non-financial and 25 financial corporations are "very powerful
indeed."[108]

Moreover, many of these corporations are foreign-owned and
controlled, which means that important decisions regarding the development
of the Canadian economy are taken outside the country. This is particularly so
in the resources and manufacturing sectors where foreign ownership levels are
very high (see Table 8-2). The implications of foreign ownership are now well
understood; they include:

- a truncated form of operations of foreign-controlled subsidiary companies
  in Canada in that they do not possess all the functions, which are normally
  part of a business such as the full range of management functions and
  research and development;

- the production of the same range of products as the parent firm, with very
  limited product and production specialization;

- import intensiveness through intra-corporate transfer of goods from the
  parent to the subsidiary and hence limited linkages to Canadian suppliers;

- artificial transfer-pricing policies to favour the parent company; and

- extra-territorial expression of the laws of the country in which the parent is located.

Unique levels of foreign-ownership have profoundly influenced the structure of the Canadian economy. The "branch-plant" phenomenon has limited Canadian industrial development.

TABLE 8-2
Degree of Foreign Control of Corporations in
Selected Industry Groups in Canada

	Percent Foreign Assets		Percent Total Sales	
	1973	1980	1973	1980
Major Industry Group				
Agriculture, Forestry and Fishing	10	4	8	4
Metal Mining	45	31	43	40
Mineral Fuels	75	53	87	74
Other Mining	55	40	60	42
Total Mining	58	45	61	59
Manufacturing				
Food	48	29	38	27
Rubber Products	93	91	91	90
Textile Mills	60	54	57	54
Wood Industries	29	19	23	17
Paper and Allied Industries	45	35	45	38
Primary Metals	16	13	20	15
Metal Fabricating	44	34	45	37
Machinery	70	52	71	59
Transport Equipment	81	71	90	84
Electrical Products	65	54	68	62
Nonmetallic Mineral Products	66	70	54	60
Petroleum and Coal Products	99	70	99	82
Chemical and Chemical Products	79	77	84	76
Miscellaneous Manufacturing	50	43	52	42
Total Manufacturing	56	48	57	51
Construction	15	10	12	8
Total Utilities	10	7	11	7
Wholesale Trade	32	24	29	27
Retail Trade	19	13	17	12
Services	26	15	24	16
Total nonfinancial Industries	34	27	37	32

Source: CALURA, Report for 1980, pp. 148-9, 146-7.

As well, as noted by John K. Galbraith, large corporations do not operate strictly by the laws of the market—the aim is to control the market rather than be affected by the vagaries of the marketplace.[109] Only smaller firms operate in the traditional marketplace.

Because of the monopoly or oligopoly power of large firms, government has had to set in place a regulatory framework within which some of these firms are permitted to operate (e.g. CRTC versus Bell Telephone). However, regulatory bodies are part of the government managerial system[110] and as such come under political influence. Given the power of large firms, regulatory bodies find themselves in constant tension in their attempts to reconcile the public interest with private concerns.

The accepted view of the role of the corporate sector in Canada is possibly best summed up by the Royal Commission on Corporate Concentration:

> "In summary, the influences that have shaped the Canadian economy have made a high degree of concentration inevitable. If changes occur they are likely to be in the direction of more rather than less concentration, chiefly because of international competitive influences. Public responses to concentration should recognize that profound and far-reaching changes are not practicable. The best mix of benefits and burdens should be sought through vigilance and the selective use of the appropriate instruments of public policy. While we have recommended a number of improvements, we conclude that no radical changes in the laws governing corporate activity are necessary at this time to protect the public interest.[111]

c) Labour and Economic Development

In Canada, strikes and lockouts form an integral part of the collective bargaining process. Compared to most other Western industrialized countries, Canada tends to have fewer, but much longer strikes[112] which is why we rank high in international strike statistics.

Big unions are out to wield their power. The attitudes of unions in the face of large corporations was expressed as follows by Peter Warrian of the United Steelworkers of America:

> "It's been said that the Inco workers were crazy to strike when the company had a stockpile as high as the Rocky Mountains. But that's not what the strike was about. The strike, essentially, was about what its like to work for Inco. The people there felt oppressed and manipulated and squashed by the corporation and by the impact of economic forces over which they had no control, no meaningful say. The strike was about power and how economic decision-making is handled."[113]

Of course, on-going tensions between labour and management adversely affect productivity and Canada's international competitiveness. A recent study has found that the countries most successful in fighting inflation and unemployment (i.e.—Germany, Holland, Sweden, Austria, Norway) are those that have a high degree of "social consensus" where the unions view themselves as "social partners."[114] In these countries long-run strike activity is very low (see Table 8-3) and annual wage bargaining is synchronized. Barber and McCallum go on to conclude that while these social democratic countries (i.e.—large governments—see Table 7-3) manage their economic affairs well, Canada needs wage and price controls because there is no such social consensus.

d) Towards Social Consensus

Canadians have realized for some time that a social consensus would be desirable. In Canada this means tripartism; an agreement among government, business and labour on the direction of Canadian economic policy. Proposals have been advanced, but we are still far from European-type consensus.

At its May 1976 convention the Canadian Labour Congress (CLC) adopted a Manifesto that advocated a form of tripartism:

> "Logic drives us to the conclusion that the government is moving into a new era in which the institutions of this country are going to change. National planning on social and economic issues demand strong central powers. The question for the CLC is whether it wishes to be in the forefront in planning the structure of the future in the way in which it believes will best serve the workers' interests or not. The game is dangerous but the stakes are high. It is really not a question of "co-operating" with the government but one of strength and bargaining ability of which the labour movement has both."[115]

The CLC's conditions for tripartism were full partnership status with government and business and that business management give up its unilateral right to determine investment and pricing policies. In July 1976 the CLC proposed the creation of a new tripartite council for economic and social planning, which would be responsible to Parliament; a council which would have administrative, regulatory and expenditure powers much beyond the consultative process embedded in the Economic Council. It is evident that such a proposal created reservations with both business and government.

However, in the October 1976 Speech from the Throne the Government recognized the need to move towards accommodation:

> "It is essential to the enhancement of unity, equality of opportunity and individual freedom that Canadians work together in a spirit of co-operation and mutual respect. To that end, it is important for all participants to have a well defined view of their respective roles in the pursuit of national objectives."

TABLE 8-3
Selected Indicators Relating to Social Consensus,
Eighteen OECD Countries

	Strike volume (days lost per 1,000 employees), 1950-69	Standardized unemployment rate, 1965-79	Size of government, 1974-76	Index of inequality
Group I				
Switzerland	4	—	31.3	—
Netherlands	19	2.4	50.9	1.1
Germany	31	1.8	40.9	7.9
Austria	39	1.7	38.8	—
Sweden	35	2.0	48.3	2.1
Norway	108	1.7	43.5	2.9
Denmark	114	—	44.0	—
Belgium	237	4.0	40.4	—
Mean	73	2.3	42.3	3.5
Group II				
Japan	171	1.5	24.2	4.4
Group III				
New Zealand	172	—	34	—
UK	147	4.0	39.5	4.4
Australia	241	3.2	30.4	7.4
Ireland	442	—	47.6	—
US	505	5.3	29.2	8.4
Canada	435	5.7	37.7	6.3
Mean	324	4.5	36.4	6.6
Group IV				
France	243	3.2	37.8	10.0
Finland	629	3.2	35.7	—
Italy	712	6.0	40.9	—
Mean	528	4.1	28.1	10.0

Notes: 1. Size of government is defined as total non-defense spending (all levels) as a percentage of GDP.

2. Index of inequality is based on the spread of post-tax personal income adjusted for differences in household size. High values indicate high degrees of inequality.

Source: Barber, McCallum, op. cit., p.10.

An offshoot of that Speech from the Throne was a federal Working Paper entitled "The Way Ahead: A Framework for Discussion," which picked up the theme of a mixed economy involving all participants, while including a commitment to the market economy. This ambivalence continues to this day in Canadian economic policy making.

The insight of Robert Heilbroner,[116] regarding the future of the capitalist system, gives some indication on how the Canadian ambivalence could eventually be resolved. He points out that low wage countries are taking over jobs in the industrialized countries: "This is all very well for the consumer, but it is not so well for the producer. A successful social structure must ultimately support its producers over its consumers. . . . The flag of free trade will be hauled down in the coming restructuring." He goes on to conclude:

"I have done no more than sketch the general kinds of changes I think will be needed to set a successful new structure of growth in place. I suppose it can be succinctly described as a movement toward state capitalism or, perhaps more accurately, as a movement toward a capitalism in which the line that divides the economy from the polity is redrawn in favour of the polity."

And of course Canada has practised state capitalism for some time.

A shift from an adversarial to an accommodating structure would only benefit the proper allocation of financial resources and the use of natural resources. But there is no assurance that such a shift of attitude will come about soon enough to permit economic restructuring with minimal stress, if at all. This will likely mean more government intervention and associated state capitalism with all the hauling and pulling that that entails.

References

105. See for example Bailey A.R. and Hull D.G.; The Way Out; IRPP 1980. These authors argue for a more revenue dependent public sector.
106. For a detailed treatment of economic policy making see R. French: How Ottawa Decides; CIEP 1980.
107. Tupper A. and Doern B. (ed); "Public Corporations and Public Policy in Canada." IRPP 1981.
108. Jones J.C.H. and Landadio L.; in "Perspectives on the Royal Commission on Corporate Concentration"; IRPP 1979 p.79.
109. Galbraith J.K.; The New Industrial State; Signet 1967.
110. Doern B. and Aucoin P.; Public Policy in Canada; Macmillan 1979; p.184.
111. Report of the Royal Commission on Corporate Concentration, March 1978 p.413.
112. Crispo J. in The Canadian Economy—Problems and Options (ed. R. Belland and W. Pope) McGraw-Hill Ryerson Ltd. 1981 p.287.
113. Warrian P.; in "Institutions in Crisis": Couchiching Institute on Public Affairs; Yorkminster Publishing Limited 1980 p.73.

114. Barber C. and McCallum J.; Controlling Inflation, CIEP 1982.
115. Canadian Labour Congress; "Labour's Manifesto for Canada," Ottawa 1976.
116. Heilbroner R.L.; "Does Capitalism have a Future": New York Times Magazine, Aug. 15, 1982.

9. An Alternative Path for Canada

Because of Canada's long economic history of doing what came naturally—exporting resources and importing finished goods—the conventional policy thrust is to continue doing the same, particularly since we need a large merchandise trade surplus (see Chapter 4). For example, large resource development projects were the centre piece of the Government's economic strategy for the 1980s.[117]

The thrust to exploit resources for export has been with us since the earliest days of the fur trade. Moreover, we have depended on and even vaunted, large scale resource projects throughout our history. And these projects needed state support; in some cases monopoly status. Perhaps nothing better symbolizes the continuity of this tradition than the similarities between the role of the Hudson Bay Company in the early history of Quebec and that of the James Bay Development Corporation today. Our economic development attitudes are deeply entrenched. Because we are strongly affected by resource development we do not often look at other alternatives to development. It is only when some crisis occurs, such as limitations in our oil supply, that we begin to stir.

The growing uncertainties of the 1970s have forced Canadians to examine their position in the world because they are becoming increasingly aware that they are often at the mercy of growing, unstable external forces. The OPEC oil shocks of the early 1970s and growing environmental problems, such as acid rain, have brought home the reality of limits and how we are exposed to them. This realisation is possibly the principal reason why Canadians responded favourably, in the late 1970s, to the concept of a Conserver Society as an alternative path to conventional economic development, which seemed to have reached structural limitations. As espoused by the Science Council of Canada, a Conserver Society was to build on the following principles:

- Concern for the Future (highlighting structural issues)

- Economy of Design (doing more with less)

- Diversity, Flexibility and Responsibility (based on a sound ecological principle)

- Recognition of Total Costs (to highlight the real costs of doing things); and

- Respect for the Regenerative Capacity of Biosphere (emphasis on sustainable techno-socio-economic processes)[118]

The energy crisis is perhaps the clearest example illustrating how Canadians have, and are, moving to Conserver Society principles; substitution from oil to natural gas, electricity and renewable energy forms as well as conservation of energy are very much in evidence because it is economically viable to do so for the individual.

However, such is not the case on all fronts. The acid rain question illustrates the difficulties of coming to grips with a problem generated by industry and which affects all of us. While the impact of acid rain on the biosphere is now recognized, it is difficult to make the "polluter pay";[119] the issue is multifaceted and diffuse (see Chapter 5). Traditional economic and political attitudes still govern economic decision-making even where structural limits and total costs are evident. Drawing a justifiable line between the conventional wisdom and new approaches will not be easy.

However, the economic, physical, regional, demographic, and institutional structural issues identified in the previous chapters will require new approaches, if they are to be resolved effectively. To recapitulate, these issues include the following:

- dependence on resource exports;
- stresses on the resource base and environment from continued large scale resource exploitation;
- a weak industrial base leading to high levels of imports of finished products;
- high levels of foreign-ownership leading to large capital outflows from the country;
- high level of and continuing urbanization;
- an aging society;
- regional economies;
- limits to employment appearing in the service sector;
- a growing labour force and unemployment; and
- a lack of consensus on economic development directions among the major institutional groups.

These issues are reviewed in the following sections in a manner that attempts to evaluate possible directions for the future.

a) The Question of Scale

As mentioned earlier, large scale has been synonymous with Canadian economic development. Even in the earliest days of the colonial regime, efficiency and minimization of production costs were mentioned as the principal reasons for encouraging large scale enterprise.[120] This in fact continues to this day as exemplified by the $440 billion worth of mega-projects identified by the Mega-Projects Task Force.[121]

Resource development has historically been the anchor-point for the advocacy of large scale projects. What was true for the fur trade in Canada at an earlier time is now true for petrochemical plants in Alberta:

"In the light of the considerable decrease in production costs associated with world-scale plants, it can be said that achieving world scale is a necessary condition for survival in the petrochemical industry. In the case of Alberta, which suffers from being landlocked and not close to markets, the necessity of efficient size plants is all the greater in order to ensure the viability of the industry."[122]

However, while scale still dominates resource development projects, concessions have been made to incremental approaches to full-scale development because of cost implications. For example:

- exploitation of natural gas resources from the Arctic Islands is referred to as a *pilot* project by the partners[123] even though the cost is $2(+) billion;

- Dome argues for tanker transportation of oil/gas resources from the Beaufort Sea as being incremental and therefore more flexible than a commitment to a pipeline.[124]

These concessions to incrementalism are nevertheless costly and not in the realm of what most Canadians understand as step-by-step progress. Even Tar Sands development is now being considered as being possible in incremental steps; possibly with 10,000 barrel/day plants, which are an order of magnitude smaller than the previously proposed projects that have had to be postponed. Such projects are now being considered as *demonstration* projects to validate full commercial potential. The Science Council set down a list of energy demonstration projects (see Table 9-1). By any definition such projects are still large and would result in significant socio-economic and environmental impacts. But the Canadian psyche appears to demand large scale resource development projects. However, concessions now being made to incrementalism could see the beginning of a new approach to resource development on a scale, which is well within the capabilities of Canadian engineering firms and which could minimize impacts on the environment.

While resource development is viewed as being of large, possibly excessive scale, industrial development is generally perceived as sub-critical, embryonic and tenuous. It is argued that because of the "branch plant" nature of our industrial system, there are too many firms in specific sectors resulting in fragmentation of markets and inefficiencies because of the lack of economies of scale in production. There is often the conventional wisdom that calls for free trade with the USA to force a rationalization of Canadian industry and to obtain economies of scale. However, a counter argument that

TABLE 9-1
Science Council Energy Demonstration Projects
($000 1978)

Priority Demonstration Programs	Initial Funding (First 5 years)	Total Funding (Cumulative to completion)	Total Years
Fossil Fuels			
Oil and Gas			
1. Exploration and Production of Oil and Gas in Ice-Congested Waters	81 600	176 000	10-15
2. Transportation of Hydrocarbons from the Arctic by Marine Mode	507 000	617 000	5-10
3. Ability of Exploring for and Producing Oil and Gas in Very Deep Waters	62 500	111 000	5-10
Sub-Total Oil and Gas	651 000	904 000	
Coal			
4. Fluidized Bed Technology	34 200	254 000	10-15
5. Land Reclamation after Coal is Strip-Mined	660	740	5-10
Sub-Total Coal	35 000	255 000	
Nuclear Energy			
6. Irradiated Fuel Management and Disposal System	52 000	444 600	20-25
7. Feasibility of the Thorium Cycle	95 000	1 750 000	25
Sub-Total Nuclear Energy	147 000	2 194 600	
Renewable Energy			
8. Feasibility of Generating Gaseous and Liquid Fuels from Forest and Agricultural Residues	3 950	37 000	10-15
9. Solar Water and Space Heating Systems	15 150	40 000	10-15
10. Energy Generation from Solid Wastes	1 510	58 000	10-15
Sub-Total Renewable Energy	20 610	136 000	
Conversion Technologies			
11. Co-Generation of Electricity and Heat	6 100	270 000	10-15
Sub-Total Conversion Technologies	6 100	270 000	
Totals	860 000	3 760 000	

Source: Science Council of Canada; Roads to Energy Self-Reliance; Report No. 30, 1979.

is advanced is that rationalization can take place within Canada without the need for free trade for the following reasons:

"First, contemporary research suggests that, excluding automobiles and petroleum products, about 70 percent of consumer products (measured by value) could be manufactured locally in optimal-sized plants if the population were about one million and about 20 percent could still be efficiently produced locally for centres of only 200,000 people. Second, it has been found that, using the conventional technology of major firms, the unit costs of production for a wide range of industries would generally rise much less than 10 percent if plants one-third the accepted minimal optimal scale were constructed. Since transportation costs from foreign places of production frequently average well above 10 percent, local factories of smaller size could be quite competitive. Third, other research suggests that cost reductions can be achieved at much smaller scale than is frequently observed. All too often, scale has been dictated by the technology of the large transnational corporation and may not be as rigid as once thought."[125]

This line of argumentation leads to the possibility of considering an industrial strategy that can be based on import substitution as well as capturing the new high-technology opportunities (e.g.—communications, mini-computers, etc.) to alleviate the massive end products deficit in our merchandise trade account (i.e.—$20 billion in 1981—see Table 4-4). If such a strategy were successful then there would be less pressure on resource exploitation to ensure a large merchandise trade surplus to offset the service deficit on current account (see Chapter 4). There are many areas where we can act to replace imports ($79 billion in 1981) particularly in end products, as indicated by Tables 9-2 and 9-3. Many economists argue that this would be an economic distortion since our comparative advantage is in resource development. However, as the Japanese have shown the world, comparative advantage can be engineered!

Moreover, the micro-electronics revolution is bringing new efficiencies to traditional production processes, which is affecting the traditional notion of economies of scale, necessitating large production runs. Automation offers great flexibility for short production runs; productivity is increased (e.g.— robotics) and efficiencies are achieved in a number of areas, such as reduced inventories. Eventually we are bound to see the fully automated factory.[126] Of course, as we move towards more and more automation, jobs will be shed and unemployment will increase, unless new employment opportunities emerge. However, as indicated in Chapter 4, there is no clear evidence as to where these opportunities will arise to meet the needs of a growing labour force as shown

TABLE 9-2
Import Profile (1981)

Category	Value ($000)	Percentage
Live Animals	201,917	0.2
Food, Beverages, Tobacco	4,979,199	6.4
Crude Materials	12,149,986	15.4
Fabricated Materials	14,529,038	18.4
End products	45,801,474	58.3
Special Transactions	1,003,434	1.3
Total	78,665,048	100

Source: Statistics Canada: Summary of External Trade, Cat #65-001 Dec. 1981.

TABLE 9-3
Percent of the Domestic Market Served by Imports
for Selected Products (1980)

Product	Import Penetration (percent)
Metal Working Machinery	89
Drilling Machinery and Drill Bits	over 90
Telecommunications and Related Equipment	63
Office Machines and Equipment	over 90
Scientific and Professional Equipment	70

Source: Based on information supplied by Statistics Canada

in Chapter 6. Capital intensity can no longer be identified principally with large scale resource projects.

It is now widely recognized that smaller firms generate jobs at a faster pace than larger firms. For example, a study of ten young electronics firms shows that:[127]

- skilled employment is produced at a rapid pace (38% per annum compounded growth rate compared to a national average of 3%);

- productivity increased at a rate of 32% per annum compounded;

- the firms are export oriented (50% of output).

These arguments are brought forward by the advocates of a technology-based industrial strategy. The Government of Quebec, on the other hand, has opted for a broader economic strategy, but still aimed at stimulating small and medium size firms (PME) for the precise reason that they generate jobs at a faster rate. The focus on smaller firms is now clearly evident in Canadian policy-making. Moreover, there is a growing literature indicating the ineffectiveness of larger firms.[128]

While jobs are created and the scale of operation in smaller firms can be more in keeping with Conserver Society principles, there is no certainty that the absolute level of job creation will be sufficient to lower the level of unemployment significantly. However, an industrial strategy aimed at maintaining the competitive edge of larger Canadian firms and at creating and encouraging small and medium size firms to replace imports on the one hand and to capture new export markets on the other, should be seriously considered. Capturing one's own domestic market becomes very important at a time of growing uncertainty in international markets.

Any industrial strategy would have to be supported by a monetary policy that favours an exchange rate that encourages exports and import substitution, as is done in other countries.

b) The Question of Employment

The demographic trends outlined in Chapter 6 suggested a growing labour force, which will find it increasingly difficult to find employment in a slow growth economy. Moreover with technology replacing labour, there is as yet no clear indication if new firms (and new employment) will come into being at a faster rate than technology is creating unemployment.[129] It is clear, however, that technology is producing major dislocations in employment patterns and opportunities.

One way of creating meaningful employment is to shift away from the concept of a *consumer society*, which has been associated with fully employed society to a *producer society* as advocated by Heilbroner (see Chapter 7). Support programs would then be aimed at supporting employment and not consumerism. Areas where employment would be directed could include:

- the development of goods and services for Third World countries which provide new market opportunities. The population of the developing world is expected to increase by some 2 billion between now and the Year 2000[130] creating new opportunities;

- the development of goods and services to ease the stresses due to expected continued urbanization, an aging society and resource development in Canada; and

- the development of industries that lead to import substitution; the development of high-technology sectors and new services as noted earlier;

In other words, stimulate employment in areas, where key structural changes are evident. Also, as exemplified by the Leontieff example in Chapter 7, shorter working time and other approaches, such as part-time work, may be needed to deal with the employment problem. It has been estimated that some 15% of employment in Canada is part-time and that most of these jobs are in the service sector,[131] in areas such as retail stores, movie theatres, restaurants and so on. The trend towards part-time work seems to be increasing, which at some point will force a rethinking of income support programs as well as the role of different approaches to work.

Of course such directions would require a rethinking of current economic policy and would necessitate sustained government support over the longer-term and the eventual consensus among the key actors responsible for the economic development process.

c) The Question of Institutions and Consensus

As mentioned in Chapter 8, the key players in Canadian economic management are government (two levels), big business and large labour unions with no consensus on economic directions among these groups. Given our history, the state of federal–provincial relations, the structure of Canadian business (e.g.—a large foreign-owned component) and the traditional posture of labour, achieving consensus may not be possible in Canada; we may be facing an intractable situation.

However, the development of institutions and processes, that could lead to some level of consensus on specific issues, is clearly a responsibility of the federal government. Moreover, the onus is on the federal government to set in place institutions that can deal effectively with micro-policies and structural issues, because of the limitations of macro-economic levers in economic management. In recent years the Federal Government has increasingly made efforts to involve other key economic actors in the decision-making process; there have been a number of federal–provincial conferences on the economy, the 23 Sector Task Forces set up by ITC in 1978, and the Major Projects Task Force, also set up in 1978, involved both business and labour in policy formulation, and ITC is merging with DREE so that the Federal Government can be more responsive to regional industrial development concerns. These are all important steps towards the development of consensus and the process should continue and become more structured over time in some kind of a formal body.

In the meantime, however, the best possible approach to maintaining cohesion and developing some level of agreement on specific issues, is for the Federal Government to develop a "web of relationships" with all key economic actors on specific issues. The reach of the Federal Government extends far afield as exemplified by the commitments extracted under the "6 & 5" wages and prices restraint program. That kind of leverage can be extended in a number of areas. For example, under the Canada Oil and Gas Act (Bill C-48), the Canada Oil and Gas Lands Administration (COGLA) is charged to extract industrial and employment benefits for Canada from frontier hydrocarbon development. In doing this COGLA must interact with the interested Provinces and Territories, the oil companies and the Canadian industrial community, that supplies goods and services, which taken together constitute an impressive network through which some consensus on frontier development may be developed. This approach can be copied throughout the economy and the various regions, including the municipal level, where the federal government has major responsibility (e.g.—airports, Post Office, CBC). For example, the pervasiveness and impact of CBC expenditures, are indicated in Table 9-4.

The Federal Government is the only locus of power, where such a strategy can be formulated, because of:

• broad regulatory powers;

• the ability to set macro-economic policies;

• the reach of federal institutions throughout Canada and abroad; and

• the necessary level of financial, intellectual and administrative resources to develop and implement such a strategy.

However, to be able to operate effectively, the Federal Government would need to have a much greater commitment to "indicative planning" for the longer term than exists at the moment, since the fundamental problems are structural and can only be resolved over the longer term. A forward-looking perspective is therefore needed to address these issues.

The experience of other countries vis-à-vis "indicative planning" is worth reviewing in this context. In *France* "indicative planning" began in 1947 with the publication of plans that projected future economic activity and identified strategic sectors as a guide to business planning. Firms were encouraged to negotiate "development contracts" with the government in strategic sectors, which set specific goals for sales, exports and jobs. Companies that made such commitments received tax incentives, subsidized loans and other official aid. Current strategic sectors include electronic office equipment, energy-saving equipment, oceanographic equipment, bio-technology and industrial robots. In this way France is able to restructure its industrial base. Since there is on-going discussion among government, business and labour on successive plans, some social consensus has developed on economic directions over the years.

In *Japan*, the Ministry of International Trade & Industry (MITI) produces various planning documents based on inputs from all sectors of society, including consumers. The documents reflect broad consensus and are used as guides to investment decisions and government support in the specific sectors identified. For the 1980s the strategic areas include optical fibres, ceramics, high-efficiency resins, solar energy, deep geothermal power generation, ultra-high-speed computers, space and ocean development.

TABLE 9-4
Impact of CBC Expenditures on National Economic Activity and Employment

Province	Expenditures 79/80 ($000)	Economic Activity Generated*	CBC Employment (no. of employees)	Indirect Employment Generated by CBC expenditures* (man-years)	Multiplier
Nfld/Lab	14,552	24,145	356	252.4	1.66
Nova Scotia	15,750	38,640	419**	464.3	2.45
P.E.I.	2,390	5,740	58***	60.5	2.40
New Brunswick	10,478	28,039	256**	358.9	2.68
Quebec	205,579	582,272	4,621	6,747.8	2.83
Ontario	255,567	793,802	4,402	9,983.5	3.11
Manitoba	20,878	57,779	766	666.5	2.77
Saskatchewan	8,659	29,296		219.9	3.38
Alberta	20,424	86,756	513	471.4	4.25
B.C.	30,042	77,990	637	837.4	2.60
NWT/Yukon	6,693	10,409	148	139.3	1.56
Corp. Adjustment	6,305	—	—	—	—
Foreign	4,832	—	—	—	—
CANADA	602,149	1,734,868	12,187	20,472.0	2.88

*Obtained through Statistics Canada's Input/Output Model of the Canadian Economy
**Estimates derived from CBC Financial Statistics

Source: Nordicity Group Ltd., Study for the CBC, Dec. 1981.

While there is ambivalence in Britain regarding planning, there have been successes, where a commitment was made to "pick a winner." For example, in 1972 the UK came to the conclusion that without government intervention the country would only capture about 25% to 40% of the industrial benefits from North Sea oil and gas development. A policy was set in place to increase UK content and by 1979, the domestic share of the offshore business was 79%. UK offshore firms are now setting up ventures in Canada to exploit the industrial opportunities related to East Coast offshore development in the 1980s and beyond. Other sectors where specific strategies have been set in place include micro-electronics and machinery.

Even in the US, despite the free market rhetoric, there is a form of planning centred on the defense industry. Because the US defense budget is so large[132] and is based on the development of strategic armaments to be built by US industry, that industry remains at the leading edge of industrial development. Moreover, the US has various "Buy American" policies to ensure the key industrial opportunities are seized by American firms.[133]

Canada has neither the large defense budget of the US nor the indicative planning framework of other countries. Given our socio-political inclinations, the latter would seem to be a more appropriate option than the former. Within the Federal Government, the obvious focal point to begin discussion of indicative economic plans is the Ministry of State for Economic and Regional Development (MSERD), the Government's economic overview body, which controls the economic development budgetary envelope. The experience of both the industrialized and developing countries[134] in "indicative planning" suggests that unless Canada adapts the concept to its own conditions, it will be relegated to undertaking those residual tasks that other countries do not want with all the associated social, economic and environmental stresses that drift entails.

As economist Lester Thurow stated:

"You have to have a goal and a strategy for reaching the goal, and that is probably the most important thing industrial policies do. It's the fact that you're forced to think about where you want to go and how you're going to get there and what goal you're really trying to reach. I think in Canada the goal ought to be: we're going to have a better economy than the American economy rather than a worse one. We're going to have more growth, less unemployment, less inflation, more productivity. Then you figure out how you get from here to there."[135]

An indicative planning process linking ends and means should become the focal point for discussion of economic policy direction.

d) Towards a Workable Future

Based on the foregoing analysis, a strategy to guide Canada to the year 2000 and beyond would include the following elements:

- establishing an indicative planning mechanism within the Federal Government, which involves the provinces, business and labour in discussions of our economic future;

- continued push on resource development into the medium term, accepting attendant social and environmental stresses, for balance of payment reasons;

- setting in place and sustaining a long term industrial strategy based on (a) capturing new industrial (particularly high-technology) opportunities, (b) import replacement and (c) developing goods and services related to priorities such as urbanization and an aging population. Specific areas for action should come from the indicative planning exercise.

- setting in place policies to tap Canadian capital markets more effectively and to encourage the development of Canadian-owned firms to reduce the deficit on the service account;

- developing policies that would ensure a sustainable resource base as well as support appropriate resource and industrial development and implement them as the pressure on balance of payments eases in the medium term and beyond;

- investigating new approaches to employment, such as a shorter work week, working from the home, work-sharing and so on, that maintain an acceptable standard of living.

Such a strategy attempts to achieve balanced and sustainable economic development between the two extremes of continued large scale resource development for exports and autarky while maintaining an acceptable level of employment and standard of living. This approach seeks consensus over the longer term on directions for economic development and industrial restructuring for Canada.

However Canada will be undergoing a transformation in a world that is also in transition. In the words of Robert Heilbroner:

". . . the period of change will last a long time. The passage from the world of small-scale capitalism to that of big business took more than two decades. The creation of the mixed economy and the welfare state required roughly as long. So it seems altogether possible that the next transformation will also last more than a decade—an extended period during which we can expect all the unease and dissention characteristic of times that have not discovered a consensus or concluded a social contract or forged a viable social structure of accumulation."[136]

The transition to sustainability will be wrought with stresses. But then little of quality is achieved without effort.

The structural analysis and strategic approach outlined in this study, lead essentially to two major questions:

1. How can we ensure that stresses on the resource base of Canada, in the medium term, are minimized? and

2. How can we constructively shape our policies and activities so that the productivity and resilience of our resources are sustained over the longer term?

The Government of Canada has frequently emphasized its recognition of the important role that public information and educated discussions play in policy development. As a contribution to the hoped-for public discussions, the facts, assessments and contentions assembled in this report are offered.

In trying to gain a better understanding of the issues at stake, it is to be recognized that conventional economic textbooks simply present the conceptually free operation of perfectly competitive markets as a starting point, which logically should lead to an efficient allocation of resources and thus to a greater well-being of both society and the individual. In a "perfect" economy, there would be no inflation, no unemployment, no balance of payments problems, or indeed any resource problems!

Notwithstanding the conceptual purity of these basic principles, in practice it is found that it is in effect the market imperfections that generate the many conflicts between political doctrines, which rest essentially upon different beliefs and perceptions with regard to the effectiveness of the balancing mechanism of the free market system and its operation. Indeed, a more thorough analysis of the issues does reveal that in essence both economic as well as any resource problems are simply manifestations of certain functional defects, which emerge when the conceptual idea of a free market economy is translated into practical transactions. Government is expected to ensure in these circumstances that any deficiencies in the free operations of the market place are suitably corrected.

We all know that certain costs, which may not be readily measurable or quantifiable (e.g. the value of fresh air or clean water, of aesthetics or the environment) are not taken into account in the process internal to private decision-making; they are said to be "external costs." It is considered essential, for purposes of assisting the operation of the "free market" to make external costs "transparent" so that the true costs of our actions become better appreciated and discussion of the acceptability of their costs is developed. Such efforts, in turn, could lead to new, innovative solutions to problems whose total costs are lower and possibly more acceptable than previously accepted high cost approaches.

Since total costing reveals the real costs of stresses on the resource base and the environment, it becomes a valuable tool in any efforts directed to minimize these stresses in the medium term.

References

117. Government of Canada; Economic Development for Canada in the 1980s, November 1981.
118. Science Council of Canada; Canada as a Conserver Society, Report No. 27, 1977.
119. The Inco case is well described in the EMR Report: *Mineral Policy, a Discussion Paper*, 1981, p.101.
120. Innis, H.A.: The Fur Trade in Canada: University of Toronto Press 1962.
121. A Report by the Major Projects Task Force on Major Capital Projects in Canada to the Year 2000: June 1981.
122. R.J. Abercrombie Sr. V-P, Nova Corp. in "Appropriate Scale for Canadian Industry," Proceedings of a Seminar—Science Council of Canada 1977; p.82.
123. Arctic Pilot Project led by Petro-Canada.
124. Dome Petroleum Ltd; Submission to the Special Committee of the Senate on the Northern Pipeline 1981.
125. Wilkinson B.W.; Canada in the Changing World Economy; C.D. Howe Research Institute 1980 p.159.
126. McLean J.M.; The Impact of the Microelectronics Industry on the Structure of the Canadian Economy, IRPP March 1979.
127. Toronto Stock Exchange; Nothing Ventured, 1980 p.29.
128. See for example Waterman R.H. and Peters T.S.: In Search of Excellence: Harper and Row (1983) and Naisbitt J.; Megatrends, Warner Books (1983).
129. Zeman Z.D.: The Impact of Computer/Communications on Employment in Canada; An Overview of Current OECD Debates, IRPP November 1979.
130. The Global 2000 Report to the President, Washington 1980.
131. Kettle, J.: A Briefing for Cabinet on Canada's Long Term Future; Privy Council Office 1979.
132. In 1982, the US defense budget was $196 billion (US). To place this figure in perspective, Canada's GNP was $350 billion (Cdn.) in 1982.
133. See Lazar, F.: The New Protectionism: CIEP, 1981.
134. See for example Carrere, M.H.; "Technological Development Strategies for Developing Countries," IRPP, 1979.
135. Thurow, L.; "An Immodest Proposal for Canada": Canadian Business, April 1983, p.63.
136. Heilbroner, R.L.: "Does Capitalism Have a Future?"; The New York Times Magazine; August 15, 1982.

APPENDICES

Appendix I

Canada's Balance of International Payments ($000,000)

TABLE 1

	1960	1961	1962	1963	1964	1965	1966	1967	1968	1969	1970	1971
Current Acct.												
Merchandise Trade	-148	+173	+184	+503	+701	+118	+224	+566	+1375	+825	+2917	+2563
Service Trans.												
Travel	-207	-160	-43	+24	-50	-32	-60	+423	-30	-218	-226	-202
Interest & Divid.	-485	-551	-581	-630	-678	-761	-822	-916	-906	-915	-997	-1141
Freight & Ship.	-91	-82	-86	-85	-35	-82	-65	-31	-40	-61	+37	-12
Other Ser. Trans.	-302	-308	-304	-333	-362	-326	-287	-395	-481	-492	-556	-725
Withholding Tax	—	—	—	—	—	—	—	—	—	—	—	-278
Bal. on Ser. Trans.	-1085	-1101	-1014	-1024	-1125	-1248	-1234	-919	-1457	-1686	-1742	-2398
Bal. on Goods and Ser.	-1233	-928	-830	-521	-424	-1130	-1010	-353	-82	-861	+1175	+165
Net Transfers	—	—	—	—	—	—	-152	-146	-25	-91	-115	+266
Current Acct. Bal.	-1233	-928	-830	-521	-424	-1130	-1162	-499	-107	-952	+1060	+431
Capital Acct.												
Direct Invest.	+620	+480	+400	+145	+175	+410	+785	+566	+365	+350	+590	+695
Portfolio Trans.	+217	+312	+294	-471	+645	+546	+325	-473	+1063	+1806	+563	+304
Other Long Term Move.	+92	+138	-6	+21	-70	-123	+118	+376	+241	+181	-146	-335
Bal. Long Term Cap.	+929	+930	+688	+637	+750	+833	+1228	+1415	+1669	+2337	+1007	+664
Bal. Short Term Cap.	+164	+133	+441	-3	-75	+694	-243	-395	-439	-1136	-196	+1030
Net Cap. Movements	+1093	+1063	+1129	+634	+675	+1527	+985	+1020	+1230	+1201	+811	+1694
Total Curr. & Cap. Bal.	-140	+135	+299	+113	+251	+397	-177	+521	+1123	+249	+1871	+2125
Net Errors & Omissions	+101	+157	-145	+32	+113	-239	-182	-501	-784	-219	-387	-1348
Alloc. of SDRs	—	—	—	—	—	—	—	—	—	—	+133	+119
Net Official Monetary Movements	-39	+292	+154	+145	+364	+158	-359	+20	+339	+30	+1617	+896

	1972	1973	1974	1975	1976	1977	1978	1979	1980	1981	1982
Current Acct.											
Merchandise Trade	+1857	+2735	+1689	-451	+1388	+2737	+3382	+4150	+8488	+7351	+17746
Service Trans.											
Travel	-234	-296	-284	-727	-1191	-1641	-1706	-1068	-1228	-1116	-1282
Interest & Divid.	-1048	-1260	-1553	-1953	-2498	-3644	-4393	-5241	-5384	-6474	-9303
Freight & Ship.	-74	-66	-224	-433	-150	-18	+65	+309	+536	+487	+895
Other Ser. Trans.	-884	-1027	-1215	-1108	-1417	-1616	-2111	-2980	-3760	-6045	-5633
Withholding Tax	-287	-322	-430	-465	-504	-534	-582	-754	-995	-1110	-1178
Bal. on Ser. Trans	-2527	-2971	-3706	-4686	-5760	-7453	-8727	-9734	-10831	-14258	-16501
Bal. on Goods and Ser.	-670	-235	-2017	-5137	-4372	-4716	-5345	-5584	-2343	-6907	+1245
Net Transfers	+284	+344	+557	+380	+530	+417	+43	+690	+1247	+1561	+1424
Current Acct. Bal.	-386	+108	-1460	-4757	-3842	-4299	-5302	-4894	-1096	-5346	+2669
Capital Acct.											
Direct Invest.	+220	+69	+35	-190	-890	-115	-2135	-1675	-2565	-10500	-1225
Portfolio Trans.	+1596	+659	+1772	+4477	+8654	+5355	+5081	+3324	+5035	+10531	+11279
Other Long Term Move.	-228	-91	-766	-352	+159	-852	+333	+450	-1563	+527	-1493
Bal. Long Term Cap.	+1588	+623	+1041	+3935	+7923	+4388	+3279	+2099	+907	+558	+8561
Bal. Short Term Cap.	+472	-553	+1310	+1620	+99	+341	+461	+6752	-730	+15072	-9411
Net Cap. Movements	+2060	+75	+2351	+5555	+8022	+4729	+3740	+8851	+177	+15630	-850
Total Curr. & Cap. Bal.	+1674	+183	+891	+798	+4180	+430	-1562	+3957	-919	+10284	+1819
Net Errors & Omissions	-1455	-652	-867	-1203	-3658	-1851	-1737	-2268	-578	-9068	-2514
Alloc. of SDRs	+117	—	—	—	—	—	—	+219	+217	+210	—
Net Official											
Monetary Movements	+336	-467	+24	-405	+522	-1421	-3299	+1908	-1280	+1426	-695

Source: Statistics Canada, *The Canadian Balance of International Payments*, cat. 67-201 and 67-001, various years.

Appendix II

Canada's Commodity Trade ($000,000)

TABLE 1

	1960	1961	1962	1963	1964	1965	1966	1967	1968	1969	1970	1971
1. AGRICULTURAL												
Exports	988.0	1264.7	1240.1	1461.8	1840.4	1708.9	1966.3	1644.6	1613.1	1464.2	1868.5	2102.6
Imports	582.3	628.8	664.4	780.2	794.7	769.7	804.6	1883.5	918.1	1062.6	1115.5	1156.8
Balance	+405.7	+635.9	+575.7	+681.6	+1045.7	+939.2	+1161.7	+761.1	+695.0	+401.6	+753.0	+945.8
2. CRUDE MATERIALS												
Exports	1114.5	1195.4	1361.6	1425.9	1616.1	1763.7	1947.6	2108.3	2467.6	2457.9	3068.2	3232.0
Imports	745.2	762.8	826.5	896.3	960.7	1006.3	1023.2	1062.3	1126.7	1085.5	1171.8	1321.7
Balance	+369.3	+432.6	+535.1	+529.6	+655.4	+757.4	+924.4	+1046.0	+1340.9	+1372.4	+1896.4	+1910.3
3. FABR. MATERIALS												
Exports	2727.9	2777.3	2907.1	3106.9	3502.5	3728.8	4012.1	4229.3	4855.1	5162.7	5866.4	5784.8
Imports	1334.9	1388.2	1488.8	1571.0	1813.0	2114.4	2233.1	2310.2	2434.5	2905.3	2885.4	3140.2
Balance	+1393.0	+1389.1	+1418.3	+1535.9	+1689.5	+1614.4	+1779.0	+1919.1	+2420.6	+2257.4	+2981.0	+2644.6
4. END PRODUCTS												
Exports	411.2	505.6	654.8	779.1	1109.0	1300.1	2119.3	3115.9	4277.5	5378.2	5566.8	6170.7
Imports	2726.4	2887.3	3150.6	3172.4	3701.2	4476.3	5483.4	6550.0	7619.5	8884.9	8617.7	9820.7
Balance	-2315.2	-2381.7	-2495.8	-2393.3	-2592.2	-3176.2	-3364.1	-3434.1	-3342.0	-3506.7	-3050.9	-3650.0
5. TOTAL TRADE*												
Exports	5255.6	5755.0	6178.5	6798.5	8094.2	8525.1	10070.6	11120.7	13250.9	14498.2	16401.1	17320.8
Imports	5482.7	5768.6	6257.8	6558.2	7487.7	8633.1	9866.4	11075.2	12358.0	14130.4	13951.9	15606.6
Balance	-227.1	-13.6	-79.3	+240.3	+606.5	-108.0	+204.2	+45.5	+892.9	+367.8	+2449.2	+1714.2

*Includes Special Transactions

	1972	1973	1974	1975	1976	1977	1978	1979	1980	1981	1982
1. AGRICULTURAL											
Exports	2355.1	3156.5	3837.2	4062.6	4275.1	4545.8	5285.4	6313.8	8214.8	9404.8	10219.7
Imports	1400.5	1981.5	2513.8	2694.8	2871.0	3307.7	3768.6	4236.4	4802.8	5181.1	4939.3
Balance	+954.6	+1175.0	+1323.4	+1367.8	+1404.1	+1238.1	+1516.8	+2077.4	+3412.0	+4223.7	+5280.4
2. CRUDE MATERIALS											
Exports	3559.6	5024.3	7768.1	7953.6	8274.0	8849.8	8809.4	12537.8	14756.2	15168.1	14760.4
Imports	1539.8	2016.2	4072.4	5078.1	5091.1	5305.8	5853.8	7970.1	11335.4	12150.0	8672.9
Balance	+2019.8	+3008.5	+3695.7	+2875.5	+3182.9	+3544.0	+2955.6	+4567.7	+3420.8	+3018.1	+6087.5
3. FABR. MATERIALS											
Exports	6568.0	8223.9	10638.4	9796.0	12189.1	14924.8	18873.2	24375.6	29333.9	30534.6	27883.0
Imports	3579.0	4281.5	6481.7	5953.8	6210.9	6998.9	8734.8	12023.9	12700.7	14529.0	11794.4
Balance	+2989.0	+3942.3	+4156.7	+3842.2	+5978.2	+7925.9	+10138.4	+12351.7	+16633.2	+16005.6	+16088.6
4. END PRODUCTS											
Exports	7136.2	8386.2	9088.6	10097.3	12708.0	15117.2	18538.8	20923.8	21726.3	25129.0	28336.9
Imports	11947.7	14797.4	18282.1	20610.1	22776.1	26122.2	30752.6	38073.5	39525.6	45801.5	40932.9
Balance	-4811.5	-6411.2	-9193.5	-10512.8	-10068.1	-11005.0	-12213.7	-17149.7	-17799.3	-20672.5	-12596.0
5. TOTAL TRADE*											
Exports	19660.7	24836.9	31411.9	31995.7	37575.7	43505.8	51681.4	64317.3	74259.3	80895.2	81464.0
Imports	18669.4	23323.5	31639.4	34667.6	37444.4	42156.0	49605.9	62870.7	69127.6	78665.0	67355.3
Balance	+991.3	+1513.4	-227.5	-2671.9	+131.3	+1349.8	+2075.5	+1446.6	+5131.7	+2230.2	+14108.7

*Includes Special Transactions
Source: Statistics Canada, *Summary of External Trade*, cat. # 65-001 and 65-201, various years.

Appendix III

Balance Of Trade In
End Products

TABLE 1
Balance of Trade in Highly Research Intensive Products
($000,000)

Year	Chem.	Mach.	Electr.	Aircraft	Sc & Prof. Equip.	Total High Research Intensity
1966	-241	-1274	-356	+64	-191	-1998
1967	-247	-1203	-355	+73	-220	-1952
1968	-307	-1251	-303	+10	-263	-2114
1969	-352	-1443	-443	+1	-301	-2538
1970	-368	-1409	-341	+46	-304	-2376
1971	-352	-1489	-537	+80	-364	-2662
1972	-473	-1868	-772	+224	-432	-3321
1973	-604	-2248	-944	-53	-535	-4384
1974	-953	-2914	-1173	-173	-674	-5887
1975	-907	-3373	-1122	-197	-735	-6334
1976	-915	-3550	-1459	+116	-771	-6579
1977	-971	-3649	-1695	+155	-985	-7145
1978	-939	-4300	-1910	-35	-1272	-8452
1979	-868	-5693	-2200	-226	-1490	-10477
1980	-527	-6864	-2196	-271	-1628	-11486
1981	-439	-7549	-2559	-328	-1863	-12738
1982	-518	-5728	-2143	+573	-1727	-9543

Source: Industry, Trade & Commerce, *Manufacturing Trade and Measures*, 1966-82, August 1983.

TABLE 2
Balance of Trade in Medium Research Intensive Products
($000,000)

Year	Paper & Allied	Prim. Met.	Other Trans.	Petr. & Coal	Total Medium Research Intensive
1966	+1488	+756	−609	−165	+1470
1967	+1509	+957	−434	−172	+1860
1968	+1621	+1150	−277	−186	+2308
1969	+1892	+887	−59	−185	+2535
1970	+1940	+1496	+308	−151	+3593
1971	+1915	+1127	+161	−135	+3068
1972	+2040	+1074	−250	−54	+2810
1973	+2443	+1327	−540	+30	+3260
1974	+3733	+1171	−1400	+58	+3562
1975	+3495	+1358	−1700	+104	+3257
1976	+4083	+2108	−1061	+11	+5141
1977	+4557	+2363	−1039	−86	+5795
1978	+5176	+2913	−850	+306	+7545
1979	+6537	+1795	−2939	+979	+6372
1980	+7929	+4272	−2130	+962	+11033
1981	+8294	+3427	−2515	+992	+10198
1982	+7521	+4032	+2110	+816	+14,479

Source: See Table 1.

TABLE 3
Balance of Trade in Low Research Intensive Products
($000,000)

Year	Food & Bev.	Tobacco	Wood	Met. Fab.	Non-Met.
1966	+229	−2	+535	−280	−126
1967	+230	−2	+566	−304	−128
1968	+215	−2	+716	−296	−108
1969	+181	−2	+752	−368	−132
1970	+249	−2	+738	−338	−122
1971	+262	−4	+891	−356	−139
1972	+204	−3	+1228	−410	−143
1973	+284	−6	+1643	−512	−153
1974	−30	−5	+1223	−655	−238
1975	+27	−10	+899	−717	−284
1976	+35	−9	+1686	−757	−311
1977	+207	−8	+2577	−795	−308
1978	+281	−10	+3557	−883	−249
1979	+607	−11	+4213	−944	−285
1980	+709	−13	+3740	−1017	−444
1981	+1260	−15	+3366	−1151	−465
1982	+1380	−22	+3433	−914	−321

Year	Rubber & Plast.	Textiles	Furn. & Fix	Total Balance
1966	−95	−353	−19	−111
1967	−95	−331	−22	−86
1968	−140	−332	−24	+29
1969	−175	−386	−16	−146
1970	−155	−364	−6	0
1971	−194	−391	−10	+59
1972	−234	−527	−30	+85
1973	−273	−620	−53	+310
1974	−514	−758	−102	−1079
1975	−465	−694	−95	−1339
1976	−322	−829	−126	−633
1977	−467	−826	−129	+251
1978	−491	−968	−123	+1114
1979	−581	−1226	−92	+1681
1980	−551	−1063	−45	+1316
1981	−480	−1249	−61	+1205
1982	−185	−988	+61	+2430

Source: See Table 1

TABLE 4
No Research At All
($000,000)

Year	Leather	Knit Mill	Clothing	Printing	Other	Total No Research Trade Balance
1966	–43	–34	–35	–150	–163	–425
1967	–45	–37	–41	–168	–191	–482
1968	–63	–60	–49	–190	–219	–581
1969	–73	–79	–40	–215	–252	–659
1970	–80	–98	–30	–221	–244	–673
1971	–98	–156	–29	–232	–254	–769
1972	–124	–186	45	–245	–355	–955
1973	–132	–175	–54	–275	–466	–1102
1974	–184	–205	–94	–318	–594	–1395
1975	–241	–266	–140	–378	–639	–1664
1976	–288	–333	–297	–397	–757	–2072
1977	–300	–300	–222	–474	–850	–2146
1978	–331	–306	–217	–555	–947	–2356
1979	–409	–346	–300	–682	–1033	–2770
1980	–374	–337	–244	–719	–981	–2655
1981	–475	–381	–331	–813	–1126	–3126
1982	–446	–366	–390	–884	–1050	–3136

Source: See Table 1.

TABLE 5
Total Trade Balance in Manufactured Products
($000,000)

1966	−1063
1967	−661
1968	−359
1969	−809
1970	+453
1971	−464
1972	−1378
1973	−1914
1974	−4799
1975	−6081
1976	−4141
1977	−3287
1978	−2153
1979	−5195
1980	−1792
1981	−4462
1982	+4230

Source: See Table 1.

Appendix IV

Employment and GDP Statistics

TABLE I
Employment—Canada
(000)

	Resources	Manufacturing	Services	Total
1960	891	1419	3269	5965
1961	865	1452	3361	6055
1962	838	1502	3491	6225
1963	826	1552	3590	6375
1964	825	1650	3723	6609
1965	828	1636	3934	6862
1966	766	1744	4143	7152
1967	777	1756	4371	7379
1968	784	1753	4547	7537
1969	752	1819	4728	7780
1970	729	1768	4955	7919
1971	735	1766	5114	8104
1972	697	1923	5330	8344
1973	693	1927	5602	8761
1974	703	1978	5858	9125
1975	703	1871	6108	9284
1976	707	1921	6216	9479
1977	705	1888	6422	9648
1978	731	1956	6653	9972
1979	756	2070	6904	10369
1980	773	2105	7158	10655
1981	798	2120	7370	10933
1982	726	1926	7331	10574
1983	757	1886	7525	10734
Average Annual Rate of Growth	-.6%	1.4%	5.7%	3.5%

Source: Statistics Canada, *Historical Labour Force Statistics*, cat. 71-201, various years.

Global 2000: Canada

TABLE II
Employment Distribution—Canada
(percent)

	Resources	Manufacturing	Services	Total*
1960	14.9	23.8	54.8	100.0
1961	14.3	23.9	55.5	100.0
1962	13.5	24.1	56.1	100.0
1963	12.9	24.3	56.3	100.0
1964	12.5	25.0	56.3	100.0
1965	12.1	23.8	57.3	100.0
1966	10.7	24.4	57.9	100.0
1967	10.5	23.8	59.2	100.0
1968	10.4	23.2	60.3	100.0
1969	9.7	23.4	60.8	100.0
1970	9.2	22.3	62.6	100.0
1971	9.1	21.8	63.1	100.0
1972	8.3	21.8	63.9	100.0
1973	7.9	22.0	63.9	100.0
1974	7.7	21.6	64.2	100.0
1975	7.6	20.1	65.8	100.0
1976	7.5	20.3	65.6	100.0
1977	7.3	19.6	66.6	100.0
1978	7.3	19.6	66.7	100.0
1979	7.3	20.0	66.6	100.0
1980	7.2	19.7	67.2	100.0
1981	7.3	19.4	67.4	100.0
1982	6.9	18.2	69.3	100.0
1983	7.0	17.6	70.1	100.0

*includes construction
Source: See Table I.

TABLE III
Gross Domestic Product By Industry—Canada
($1971 000,000)

	Resources	Manufacturing	Services	Total*
1960	4371.3	9958.4	28923.3	46958.9
1961	4124.8	10358.2	29921.2	47864.8
1962	4678.9	11310.3	31463.9	51288.5
1963	5045.8	12071.9	33015.3	54119.3
1964	5008.4	13233.4	35292.9	57782.8
1965	5234.2	14433.0	37568.3	62029.1
1966	5687.8	15518.3	39818.4	66192.1
1967	5394.4	15975.3	42149.9	68523.3
1968	5811.3	16965.4	44303.0	72353.4
1969	6013.3	18241.2	47036.1	76766.2
1970	6351.6	17993.6	48843.6	78597.9
1971	6659.0	19040.9	51714.2	83260.5
1972	6525.2	20516.3	55080.6	88143.1
1973	7229.1	22674.0	58923.4	95028.4
1974	6883.1	23497.2	62520.6	99347.2
1975	6732.7	22122.5	64647.8	100282.6
1976	7041.1	23431.9	67784.4	105249.4
1977	7311.2	23901.6	70271.8	108340.8
1978	6986.0	25139.9	73125.9	111957.9
1979	6961.0	26631.8	75664.8	116145.4
1980	7294.4	25846.3	77059.1	117059.0
1981	7427.7	26378.5	79395.2	120545.6
1982	6944.3	23066.7	78878.4	115530.0

*includes construction

Source: Unpublished data available from Statistics Canada, Cansim Matrix
000389.

TABLE IV
Canada
Distribution of Gross Domestic Product by Industry ($ 1971)
(percent)

	Resources	Manufacturing	Services
1960	9.3	21.2	61.6
1961	8.6	21.6	62.5
1962	9.1	22.0	61.3
1963	9.3	22.3	61.0
1964	8.7	22.9	61.1
1965	8.4	23.3	60.6
1966	8.6	23.4	60.2
1967	7.9	23.3	61.5
1968	8.0	23.4	61.2
1969	7.8	23.8	61.3
1970	8.1	22.9	62.1
1971	8.0	22.9	62.1
1972	7.4	23.3	62.5
1973	7.6	23.9	62.0
1974	6.9	23.6	62.9
1975	6.7	22.1	64.5
1976	6.7	22.3	64.4
1977	6.7	22.1	64.9
1978	6.2	22.4	65.3
1979	6.0	22.9	65.1
1980	6.2	22.1	65.8
1981	6.2	21.9	65.9
1982	6.0	20.0	68.3

Source: Based on data available from Statistics Canada.

TABLE V
Canada
Index of Real Domestic Product by Industry
1960 = 100.0

	Resources	Manufacturing	Services	Total
1960	100.0	100.0	100.0	100.0
1961	94.4	104.0	103.4	101.9
1962	107.0	113.6	108.8	109.2
1963	115.4	121.2	114.1	115.2
1964	114.6	132.9	122.0	123.0
1965	119.7	144.9	129.9	132.1
1966	130.1	155.8	137.7	140.9
1967	123.4	160.4	145.7	145.9
1968	132.9	170.4	153.2	154.1
1969	137.6	183.2	162.6	163.5
1970	145.3	180.7	168.9	167.4
1971	152.3	191.2	178.9	177.3
1972	149.3	206.0	190.4	187.7
1973	165.4	227.7	203.7	202.3
1974	157.5	235.9	216.1	211.6
1975	154.0	222.1	223.5	213.5
1976	161.1	235.3	234.3	224.1
1977	167.2	240.0	242.9	230.7
1978	159.6	252.4	252.8	238.4
1979	159.2	267.4	261.6	247.3
1980	166.9	259.5	266.4	249.3
1981	169.9	264.9	274.5	256.7
1982	158.9	231.6	272.7	246.0

Average Annual
Rate of Growth

	2.7%	6.0%	7.8%	6.6%

Source: See Table III

Global 2000: Canada

TABLE VI
Canada
GDP by Revised Industry Groups
($1971 000,000)

	Resource Based	Secondary Manufacturing	Services	Total*
1960	9115.4	5214.3	28923.3	46058.9
1961	9066.5	5416.5	29921.2	47874.8
1962	9947.2	6042.0	31463.9	51288.5
1963	10586.0	6531.7	33015.3	54288.5
1964	11034.6	7207.2	35292.9	57782.8
1965	11606.5	8060.7	37568.3	62029.1
1966	12394.6	8811.5	39818.4	66192.1
1967	12146.5	9223.2	42149.9	68523.3
1968	12912.8	9863.9	44303.0	72353.4
1969	13467.3	10787.2	47036.1	76766.2
1970	13939.1	10406.1	48843.6	78597.9
1971	14542.2	11157.7	51714.2	83260.5
1972	14901.1	12140.4	55080.6	88143.1
1973	16226.7	13676.4	58923.4	95028.4
1974	16106.3	14274.0	62520.6	99347.2
1975	15163.4	13691.8	64647.8	100282.6
1976	16071.1	14402.9	67784.4	105249.4
1977	16575.4	14637.4	70271.8	108340.8
1978	16710.0	15415.9	73125.9	111957.9
1979	16977.0	16615.8	75664.8	116145.4
1980	17290.7	15850.0	77059.1	117059.0
1981	17433.1	16373.1	79395.2	120545.6
1982	15789.0	14222.0	78878.4	115530.0

*includes construction
Source: see Table III

TABLE VII
Distribution of GDP by Revised Industry Group
($1971)
(percent)

	Resource Based	Secondary Manufacturing	Services
1960	19.4	11.1	61.6
1961	18.9	11.3	62.5
1962	19.4	11.8	61.3
1963	19.5	12.1	61.0
1964	19.1	12.5	61.1
1965	18.7	13.0	60.6
1966	18.7	13.3	60.1
1967	17.7	13.4	61.5
1968	17.8	13.6	61.2
1979	17.5	14.0	61.3
1970	17.7	13.2	62.1
1971	17.5	13.4	62.1
1972	16.9	13.8	62.5
1973	17.1	14.4	62.0
1974	16.2	14.4	62.9
1975	15.1	13.6	64.5
1976	15.3	13.7	64.4
1977	15.3	13.5	64.9
1978	14.9	13.8	65.3
1979	14.6	14.3	65.1
1980	14.8	13.5	65.8
1981	14.5	13.6	65.9
1982	13.7	12.3	68.3

Source: see Table III

TABLE VIII
Canada
GDP In Non-Auto Related Manufacturing Industries
Expressed as a Percent of Total GDP

	Secondary Manufacturing Autos	Total GDP	Percent
1960	4781.0	46958.9	10.2
1961	4996.1	47874.8	10.4
1962	5522.6	51288.5	10.8
1963	5884.9	54119.3	10.9
1964	6504.2	57782.8	11.2
1965	7156.0	62029.1	11.5
1966	7840.0	66192.1	11.8
1967	8081.4	68523.3	11.8
1968	8487.2	72353.4	11.7
1969	9212.0	76766.2	12.0
1970	9053.8	78597.9	11.5
1971	9464.8	83260.5	11.4
1972	10217.6	88143.1	11.6
1973	11214.7	95028.4	11.8
1974	11745.0	99347.2	11.8
1975	11194.2	100282.6	11.2
1976	11601.6	105249.4	11.0
1977	11593.3	108340.8	10.7
1978	12368.1	111957.9	11.0
1979	13555.6	116145.4	11.8
1980	13566.8	117059.0	11.6
1981	14015.3	120545.6	11.6
1982	12116.1	115530.0	10.5

Source: See Table III.